PRAISE FROM COLLEAGUES

"In this book, Tom Bird reminds us that we can do anything through ⸺⸺⸺⸺⸺⸺⸺⸺⸺⸺ and that writing is a divine w⸺

Nancy ⸺

"In *The Ca*⸺⸺⸺⸺ *Craft,* Tom Bird has conceived, written, presented, and shared with us a treasure chest about basically everything writers need to know to begin and continue their glorious journey, and reach the ultimate destination: their own published book."

Paul D. McCarthy, *New York Times* bestselling author and editor for bestselling authors Clive Cussler, Nelson DeMille, and Stephen Coonts

"A professional writer; no matter how talented, is nothing if he can't get his work published—Bird has a system."

The Pittsburgh Press

"Tom is definitely one of the holders of the vision."

Carol Adrienne, author of *The Purpose of Your Life* and *The Tenth Insight* (with James Redfield)

"Even Stephen King could learn something about writing from Tom."

Jean Marie Stine, author and former editor-in-chief of Tarcher Books

PRAISE FROM STUDENTS

"Thank you for showing me how to get published—over 300,000 books sold to date."

Jan Larkey, author of *Flatter Your Figure* (Simon & Schuster)

PRAISE FROM STUDENTS

"Tom Bird is not only a teacher, mentor, but he's also a guide to listen to the heart of God."

Dorothy Wilt, coauthor of *Nursing the Spirit* (American Nursing Association)

"I can't thank you enough for helping me fulfill my heart's deepest desire."

Debra Blais, author of *Letting Your Heart Sing* (Capital Books)

"The information that Tom Bird provides instills confidence and is empowering."

Mark Atkins, author of *Be Strong for Me* (Dove Books)

"This book is a must-read for everyone. Even if you have no interest in writing, I promise you, before you finish this book, you will have a desire to write. You won't be able to stop yourself."

Bonnie Sanchez, Seattle, WA

"Within four weeks I had written over 120,000 words. I had written a book! Without Tom, I never would have."

Karen Stone, Smyrna, GA

"With a highly contagious 'go-for-it' attitude, Tom Bird and his workshops are excellent guides for the author-to-be."

Rick Porrello, author of *The Rise and Fall of the Cleveland Mafia* (Barricade Books)

"When I first met Tom Bird, I was a burned-out lawyer with of dream of writing a mystery. Tom was an inspiration and an incredible mentor. His system works."

Mark Cohen, author of *The Fractal Murders* and *Bluetick Revenge* (Mysterious Press)

The Call

of the
Writer's
Craft

Writing and Selling the Book Within

TOM BIRD, creator of the Tom Bird Method™

Foreword by Paul McCarthy, *New York Times* bestselling author and editor

Avon, Massachusetts

Copyright © 2009 by Tom Bird
All rights reserved.
This book, or parts thereof, may not be reproduced in any
form without permission from the publisher; exceptions are
made for brief excerpts used in published reviews.

Published by
Adams Media, a division of F+W Media, Inc.
57 Littlefield Street, Avon, MA 02322. U.S.A.
www.adamsmedia.com

ISBN 10: 1-59869-854-0
ISBN 13: 978-1-59869-854-1

Printed in the United States of America.

J I H G F E D C B A

Library of Congress Cataloging-in-Publication Data
is available from the publisher.

This publication is designed to provide accurate and authoritative information with
regard to the subject matter covered. It is sold with the understanding that the publisher is not engaged in rendering legal, accounting, or other professional advice. If
legal advice or other expert assistance is required, the services of a competent professional person should be sought.

—From a *Declaration of Principles* jointly adopted by a Committee of the
American Bar Association and a Committee of Publishers and Associations

Many of the designations used by manufacturers and sellers to distinguish their product are claimed as trademarks. Where those designations appear in this book and
Adams Media was aware of a trademark claim, the designations have been printed
with initial capital letters.

The Tom Bird Method™ is a trademark of Tom Bird Seminars Inc. Corporation.

All sample contracts, letters, proposals, and e-mails are used by permission of the
person who wrote it.

This book is available at quantity discounts for bulk purchases.
For information, please call 1-800-289-0963.

To Skyla,

You were born to _____ (you fill in the blank, sweetheart—finding and then living your divine purpose is what we were all born to do). This life is all yours, girl. Don't live it for me or anyone else. Be your own person, make your own decisions, write it like a book for which you will forever be remembered. It's all yours. Live it to the fullest level of your God-given ability with every breath you take, with every beat of your big, loving heart. Love like there is no tomorrow. Dance with every step you take. And allow your heart to sing through every word you share. Just know that I will always be there for you in whatever way you need me to be. I love you more than words can say. Thank you for the honor of being your father . . .

-Your Dad, 4/2/09

Contents

Foreword

By Paul D. McCarthy,
New York Times hardcover bestselling author

Tom Bird's *The Call of the Writer's Craft* is an invaluable and unique book. Its authority is based in part on his almost forty years of being a professional writer and author; twenty-five years of success as a nationally recognized and celebrated teacher of writing; and remarkable creative, spiritual, and psychological imagination. With tens of thousands of his writer-students achieving "literary and personal success," the proof and value of his methods, ideas, approaches, visionary concepts, and insights are verified, and joyous.

Tom shares throughout the book the lessons he learned on his own journey from being an aspiring writer to reaching breakthrough new ways to write and to live. He also has a grand appreciation for knowing about and quoting the right books and authors, as their thinking expands and helps illuminate the often mysterious, baffling, frustrating creative process—before and after writing, when the writer continues into the publishing process.

Tom's capacity for originality, one of the major, defining aspects of true creativity, is admirable and amazing. He shares with us in this book his powerful, often life-changing new ideas and methods, and presents them with clarity, color, practicality, and really charged enthusiasm. Such profound concepts as the "Divine Author Within" are almost self-defining by title. Yet they are also so insightful, deep, and multidimensional in their nature and application that they need to be read in Tom's full expression and context to be as appreciated and useful as intended.

True to us, himself, and his guiding core concept, he doesn't even wait until the first page of Chapter 1 to prepare us for all that follows. His Introduction makes us feel as though we're having a classic "one-on-one" session with him.

His ideas, insights, and answers are intended for all the aspiring writers who, for regrettably too many reasons—mostly not of their making—haven't been able to move from aspiration to actual writing, of a book, but as is true of the entire book, Tom has excellent lessons for even veteran, established authors. His noble goal is to get us to re-learn and newly learn what we should know about how we can become writers ourselves, by removing all possible obstacles, excuses, blocks, etc. He takes us into the deepest part of our hearts and souls, to where writing begins, and has us gain a much better, stronger, motivating sense of ourselves, and the certainty of our ability to write a book.

For Tom, the fundamental, multistage, additional preparation for actually starting to write our book is of such vast importance that it comprises most of Part One. He has such inspirational confidence in our ability to do what he's guiding us through in preparation that in Chapter 7, which concludes Part One, he moves forward on the assumption that we've already written our first book, by having done what he taught us.

Maintaining the book's continuous thematic flow, Tom has us move right into the next process and goal, with Part Two's practical, wise, seasoned, and protective explanation and series of steps to "Getting Published." Even for publishing professionals, the industry and publishing process is inherently complex. What Tom does very, very well, as only an insider of his multiple experience can, is simplify, clarify, explain, and advise, so that we know why and what to do, and most importantly, do all of it *right*—the first time.

For almost all traditional book publishing, literary agents are the necessary connection between us and acquiring editors and publishers, and Tom takes considerable care and two full chapters to advise us on how to find the potential best agents and query them. His lessons and many interwoven methods and approaches are intended to help us maximize the quality and number of expressions of interest we get from agents.

When Part Two concludes and it doesn't seem possible that Tom could give us more . . . he does. In the appendices that follow, he provides very practical advice, reminders, and, once more, samples—of query letters, sample proposal packages, and *verbatim* queries to agents, and responses from those named agents.

In sum, in *The Call of the Writer's Craft,* Tom Bird has conceived, written, presented, and shared with us a treasure chest about basically everything writers need to know to begin and continue their glorious journey, and reach the ultimate destination: their own published book. With more to come.

Paul D. McCarthy
New York City
www.McCarthyCreative.com
March 17, 2009

Introduction

I CAME TO the principles that I share in this book through divine intervention.

That's right; tired of failing miserably as an aspiring writer, I was finally desperate enough to seek God's assistance.

So desperate was I that I promised to share with others whatever He/She presented so that those others wouldn't have to suffer as badly as I was at that moment. In my opinion, there's nothing worse than having a dream stuck inside of you without a route for releasing it. My dream was to write and publish books, but I just couldn't seem to make it happen.

Two nights after I made my request, I was awoken by the reply, which came in the form of a vision. In it, I saw exactly how I needed to approach both the writing of books and publishing.

That vision became the *Tom Bird Method*. Once I adapted that vision into a book idea, I was off and running. I sold the rights to my first book about six weeks later to Harper & Row, and I received an advance equivalent to three times the salary I was earning at the time.

After signing a contract with my publisher, I began work on my book. Using the principles I was shown in my vision, I wrote the 110,000-word manuscript in less than three months. Yes, you read that right. I did it while working my day job seven days a week, an average of seventeen hours a day. Shortly after completing the book,

I resigned from my position and began offering classes at local colleges and universities as a way of sharing what later became known as the Tom Bird Method.

I bet you can identify with the desperation I felt before my vision. You, too, have a book (or books) trapped inside you, calling to be written. You know they're in there, but you can't seem to get them out in an easy, free-flowing, natural way. You've probably experienced moments when you *were* able to write that effortlessly and brilliantly, but you can't seem to recapture that feeling consistently.

I have good news: this book will teach you to write that way every day, whenever you want. You don't need to wait for a mythical muse or divine intervention. When you learn how to write with ease, you, too, can write as fast as I did. In fact, you can write the first draft of a great book in *fewer than thirty days*.

> "I would rather regret the things I have done than the things I have not."
>
> Former Sedona resident and acclaimed actress Lucille Ball

You may be skeptical; I understand. After all, you've probably suffered for years with your writing—frustrated by insipid prose you've written, feeling that you need to revise it again and again to perfect it, and lacking the time in your busy life to focus on it . . . and now I'm saying you can write a great book in less than thirty days? Yes. It's possible because you already have all the inspiration, ideas, and passion you will ever need for a lifetime of writing. The problem is that they're trapped inside you along with those book(s). All I'll do is show you how to release them.

In Part I, I'll show you what goes on in your head when you try to write. Once you understand the forces at play, you can learn how to manage, balance, and tap into them. You'll begin to see why you've encountered certain problems and how to overcome them. Once we've laid this groundwork, I'll outline exactly how to write your first draft in thirty days—and how to revise it just as quickly and painlessly. In Part II, I'll explain the ins and outs of publishing basics, so you're ready when it's time to find a literary agent and sell your book. Yes, I'm *that* confident that you'll get there. Throughout the book, you'll find extra material that will give you even more useful advice:

- **Sedona Secrets:** Actions you can take to improve your writing or better understand the publishing process.
- **Pearls of Wisdom:** Insights into the writing process or publishing world.
- **Writer's Reflection:** Short exercises you can complete after you've learned a particular concept.
- **Quotes:** Peppered throughout the book are quotes from famous Sedona residents, who will offer you their experience, wisdom, and, above all, humor.
- **Divine Writer Within sections:** In these passages, I'll tell you about a student of mine who overcame a problem or used part of my method to find his or her success.

Let me help you answer the call of that book inside you . . .

"I have a great love and respect for religion, great love and respect for atheism. What I hate is agnosticism, people who do not choose."

Former Sedona resident
and acclaimed filmmaker
and actor Orson Wells

"In life, all good things come hard, but wisdom is the hardest to come by."

Former Sedona resident and
acclaimed actress Lucille Ball

part one

Thirty Days or Fewer to Write Your Book

"If the songs are not sung and myths are not told, then the land will die."

Nicholas Mann,
author of *Sedona Sacred Earth*

"I've always been really in love with the natural world, and I get a lot of inspiration from the natural world. Some of my best ideas come from being out in the wilderness."

Stanley Jordan,
renowned jazz guitarist and Sedona resident

chapter one

Begin Your Journey

"Once upon a time the Yavapai people lived in Montezuma's
Well. With the coming of the Great Flood, they knew that all
life in the underworld would be lost. So they placed a beautiful
young girl in a hollow log, along with food for the journey, a
woodpecker, and a lovely white pearl for protection. They called
her Lady of the Pearl. They sealed the log with pitch, and set
it free, with the hope that it would float up to a safe place and
she could create a new world. For forty days and nights the rain
came down, and the waters rose. Finally the rain ceased, and the
water receded. The log landed in Sedona—and the woodpecker
pecked free Lady of the Pearl. She was called to the top of Mingus
Mountain—where the Sun, struck by her beauty, shone upon
her. She went home to Sedona, and bathed in the divine waters
of Boynton Canyon. Shortly hereafter, she birthed a lovely baby
girl. This daughter became known as 'First Woman,' mother to
the Yavapai people."

—Sedona creation myth of the Yavapai

EVERY PEOPLE NEEDS its creation myths—and writers are no
different. We all have our book(s) within us, waiting to be born.
But how to free the great works trapped inside us? Where is the
woodpecker to peck out our story, the sun to make our prose sparkle,
the magical waters to bear us to the far side of the publishing shore?

In search of a creation myth that works for them, some writers develop elaborate rituals, superstitions, and strategies to get them writing—and keep them writing. Sometimes these strategies work—at least for a while—but more often they do not. Ultimately, most fail altogether.

But it doesn't have to be that way. You can accept the call to the writer's craft with the same confidence that Lady of the Pearl accepted the call to Mingus Mountain. You can write the books you were born to write as effortlessly as Lady of the Pearl gave birth to First Woman. And you can see your legacy in print as surely as First Woman saw her legacy in the Yavapai people.

As a bestselling author and teacher, I've shown tens of thousands of writers how to release the books they hold within—and get them published. In the intensive writer's retreats I conduct in my home of Sedona, I lead writers through my Tom Bird Method step by step—a journey I explore here with you in *The Call of the Writer's Craft*.

Sedona is a magical place. But you don't have to come to Sedona to harness the creative energy you need to do your best work—and get it published. This book is not about your coming to Sedona, though we would certainly love for you to visit; it's about finding your own Sedona, the one that has been waiting for you and calling out to you, potentially for so long, through the living, breathing, crying-to-be-expressed presence of your book(s).

Sedona Secret
HIRE GRAMMAR HELP

Are punctuation, spelling, and grammar important? Of course, but you can always get someone to correct them for you if you lack proficiency in any of these areas. Also, look for a truly unique book by Noah Lukeman entitled *A Dash of Style*, which illustrates for authors how to actually make the grammar and punctuation work for them. It's the first book of its type and the only one I've ever seen that hands the tools of punctuation and grammar back over to those who need it the most—authors—as opposed to having it forced upon them and their writing.

Begin Your Writer's Journey, Starting Now

The first thing you must do is this: Forget almost anything and everything you ever read, heard, or were taught about writing. Whatever you currently believe about your past, present, or future success or failure as a writer is undoubtedly false. Consider the following fallacies:

- **You need talent to write.** Nothing could be further from the truth. From my perspective as a writing teacher and author myself, talent is overrated. It couldn't hurt, I suppose, but you don't need it. What you need more than anything in your writing is heart. And everyone has a heart. We are all born equipped with what we need to express that essential aspect of ourselves. You just have to learn to connect with your *Divine Writer Within* (DWW), which I will help you do in the course of this book.
- **You need to be a genius to write well.** However smart you are, you are smart enough to write a book. In fact, the smaller amount of control given to your intellect, the greater degree of ease and success you will initially experience.
- **You need a formal education to succeed as a writer.** In fact, a tiny percentage of those who go on to literary success actually do so as a result of a degree. The education most important to a writer comes as the result of the living of life, as shown by the success of Steinbeck, Hemingway, Kerouac, Grisham, and so many others.
- **You are too young/old/whatever to succeed as an author.** No—you are not too old or too young or too white or too black or brown or yellow to write a book. Again, the one common denominator all bestselling authors share is heart. And the depth of your heart is not limited by your genetic makeup, ethnic background, age, or gender.
- **Writing is difficult, if not impossible.** Any activity approached in an improper manner is difficult, if not impossible. This book will get you on the right track right from the beginning, enabling

you to abandon any misconceptions or bad behaviors and allow you to step onto the right path.

- **Writing a book takes a long, long time—years, sometimes dozens of years.** Any activity, when approached incorrectly, takes a long time. However, as this book will show, it will not take you long to write and get your book published. Approaching your writing with this urgency is an absolute must if you ever want your writing to be both a professional and personal success.

- **You have to be highly proficient in spelling, punctuation, and grammar to be a successful writer.** There is no doubt that spelling, punctuation, and grammar are important components to succeeding as a writer, but by no means do you have to have the skills of an English teacher to succeed with writing and publishing. (If that were the case, we would have no English teachers, for they would all be authors.) Heart—not grammar—is the key to both your personal and professional success as a writer.

- **You have to pay your dues to succeed as a writer.** If you are determined to take the long way to writing and publishing your work, then you don't need this one. But follow the advice set forth in this book, and you can do it correctly, quickly, easily, and enjoyably the first time out. No dues to pay.

My role is to serve as your literary shaman and midwife. In doing so, I will offer you all the direction, assistance, and encouragement you deserve to birth that book or books that have been calling out to you—and to get them published as well, if that

Halt your resistance and the pain falls by the wayside.

is something you wish to do. I can guarantee that if you follow my instructions to the letter, whatever book or books that are presently inside you will be released in their entirety quickly, effectively, successfully, and, thus, pleasurably and that you will be moved down that road of publication as effortlessly and as swiftly as possible. However, like any good shaman/midwife will tell you, I cannot promise the process will be pain free. I *can* promise you, though, that any pain can be severely minimized if you limit your resistance to this process. For, in essence, pain is nothing more than a resistance to release.

So it is up to you whether you experience pain or how much pain you choose to undergo. The key to how much pain you choose to feel lies in your resistance to identifying the habits that have held you back as a writer and replacing them with actions, thoughts, and philosophies that will enable you to return to the natural, expressive, DWW-connected state in which all of us writers were born.

Dealing with Anxiety

If you are anything like the tens of thousands of aspiring authors I have known, you need to remember that it is always darkest before that dawn, and nowhere is that more true than in one's decision of finally taking the step to write. As a result, you may be feeling more tense than usual (something you may or may not consciously recognize), meaning:

1. You may feel irritable, resentful, mistrusting.
2. You may even have a headache or feel one coming on.
3. You may be overly critical of either me, the step you are about to take, or your actual chances of success as a writer, via a multitude of excuses.
4. You may even be feeling unusually shy.

If you have any one or more of these feelings, don't worry. It's normal to feel some apprehension,

Writer's
REFLECTION

Take a moment, right now, to ponder, address, and release how you're feeling. How do you do that? First, start out by listening to how you're feeling. Don't react to it, just listen. Then allow whatever resistance or inspiration you're feeling to flow, uncensored, onto a blank piece of lineless paper. Write until you have nothing else to express.

some resistance before taking a step with any significance. No matter how positive and proven the step—and this is the most positive step you as a writer can take!—you may feel tension. Because tension comes with change. You are about to take a major step forward, one that will lead to great change, so feeling some type of tension is normal.

The key to success is to allow yourself to *feel* and *express* any tension you may be experiencing. But do not allow yourself to *react* to it. Keep moving forward at all costs.

Your Artist/Writer's Pad

The DWW is expressive freedom personified. It knows and accepts no boundaries. Like you, it is limitless. So in releasing what it is dying to say, use a surface that mimics the expressive nature of the DWW—a large, lineless drawing pad. Time to provide that for both your DWW and yourself.

The bigger the drawing pad, the more the expressive freedom of the DWW will be mimicked, the better. Something that boasts of a strong bond would be best as well, such as a 14" × 17", 60-pound, sketchpad. You will be reminded time and time again, as your DWW is set free, that:

1. You are in charge of what you feel and how you choose to handle it.
2. You are the author of your own success.
3. And it has been no one else but yourself who has been holding you and your feelings back—isn't that a really refreshing feeling?
4. Your frustrations have transpired, of course, only because you have not properly been led to release that book(s) that calls from deep inside you, and to see it through to its destiny as a published work. All that is going to change, however, with this book.

Pushing Past Your Resistance

If you are like the majority of the tens of thousands of students who have entered my classes over the last quarter of a century, you have probably tried to write and/or publish and have met with, at best, minimal success (if any at all). Yet, you have probably experienced more than your share of success in *other* areas. So you may wonder why similar success at writing and publishing has eluded you. You may be frustrated and fearful and stressed out by this perceived failure on your part. All this frustration and fear and anxiety and stress have built up, resulting in a very high wall of resistance.

However, as you will discover, *there is never any real heat or a fire behind the smoking mirage that will confront you.* And you will see that by walking through it, you will be gifted with a very special present awaiting you on the other side—like the pot of gold at the end of a rainbow.

The theories behind the Tom Bird Method directly and proactively confront any inappropriate ideas about writing and publishing that you have acquired over the years. The method is best represented by a compilation of the following theories:

- You were born to write; otherwise you wouldn't have the urge to do so.
- Thus, you are being divinely led.
- The same goes for any desire you may have to publish as well.
- Both, in one way or another, are part of your life's purpose.
- You don't lack courage, commitment, or heart—those are not the reasons you have not succeeded up to this point. The reason you have not succeeded up to your standards is simply that you have not been exposed to the proper understandings that would release you to do so.
- Writing is an emotional art form and anything that inhibits that inspiration (such as your overly and unnecessarily developed Logical Brain, which we'll talk about soon) kills the flow and success of your writing.

- All the mistakes of your past can be healed and left behind forever by doing the write—oops— I mean "right" (or do I?)—things now.

Tools for Your Writing Journey

Writer's
REFLECTION

Take a moment to repeat the steps from the Writer's Reflection on page 7: Ponder, address, and release how you're feeling. Listen to how you're feeling. Don't react to it, just listen. Then allow whatever resistance or inspiration you're feeling to flow, uncensored, onto a large, blank piece of lineless paper. Write until you have nothing else to express.

An author's tools are simple but exact. You don't need to spend major amounts of money here, but you will need the following:

1. A drawing pad or two, like the one mentioned on page 8, preferably 14" × 17" or bigger
2. A few pens that fit your hand comfortably and, most of all, are smooth flowing
3. About two hours a day, six days a week, for the successful completion of the writing of your first book in thirty days or fewer (we'll be discussing when this time should be and how to come up with it shortly)

Please make sure that you have the pens and paper before moving on. Also, begin thinking about a strategy to get the two hours a day you need—you may need to speak to those in your family (or anyone else you are responsible to) about what you will be doing, rearrange your work schedule or your bedtime, and so on.

When Your Writer's Heart Speaks

When the heart of a writer speaks, what you hear is *voice*. Each and every person is born with a uniquely expressive voice. Much in the same way that two snowflakes are never exactly alike, no two writer's voices are alike. You already have a voice, whether you know it or not, whether it's buried under misconception or not. You may have to recover or uncover your voice, but you don't have to create a voice. You simply have to reveal it, love it, and accept it once again, as you did as a child, and allow it once again to come flowing through you.

Pearl of *Wisdom*

I came from nowhere and made it and you can too by using the method that led not only me, but thousands of my students, to succeed and to grow personally and professionally beyond our wildest dreams.

Exercise: Write from the Heart

Great writing is the result of writing from the heart. So I want you to get used to just doing that through the following exercise:

1. Clear out any distractions (you need to get used to doing this—so might as well begin by doing so now) and make some writing time for yourself.
2. Make sure that you have one of your large drawing pads and a couple of smooth-flowing pens nearby.
3. On one side of your paper, copy down the following quote.

   "Our deepest fear is not that we are inadequate. Our deepest fear is that we are powerful beyond measure. It is our light, not our darkness, that most frightens us. We ask ourselves, 'Who am I to be brilliant, gorgeous, talented, fabulous?' Actually, who are you not to be? You are a child of God. Your playing small does not serve the World.

   "There is nothing enlightening about shrinking so that other people won't feel unsure around you. We were born to make manifest the glory of God that is within us.

   "It is not just in some of us; it is in everyone. As we let our own light shine, we unconsciously give other people permission to do

the same. As we are liberated from our own fear, our presence automatically liberates others."

—MARIANNE WILLIAMSON, in her book
Reflections on the Principles of a Course in Miracles

4. When you are done copying it down, write down *as quickly as you can* (as you will see, writing fast is one of the keys to be able to write from the heart) any reactions or feelings you may have. Don't censor or discriminate against any feelings you have; just let them fly.

5. If you end up filling the page with feelings, thoughts, and reactions, continue onto another page and another page after that, if necessary. Continue reacting until you can either read or copy down the statement without feeling anything.

Once you have done that, you will be ready to move on to the next section in this book.

the divine writer within

I met Karen Stone through a lecture I gave at Emory University. Like most of those who sought out my method, Karen had wanted to write for years—decades, to be exact. Even though she had been successful at everything else she had taken on, Karen had not been able to master that which meant most to her—her writing.

Like most of those who attend my classes and retreats, she was desperate to get over whatever was holding her back from birthing her book. As a result, no matter how atypical my suggestions may have been compared to what she had been taught about writing up to this point, she embraced them, including releasing her book on large, lineless pieces of paper.

Once she got in line with the Tom Bird Method, the words just flowed, her book was released, and she was finally the author she had always wanted to be.

There was nothing wrong with Karen. She had only done what had been requested of or forced upon her, by learning an absolutely ineffective approach to writing, which in no way could have ever led her to accomplish her heartfelt writing goals.

Karen said, "Within four weeks I had written over 120,000 words. I had written a book. It had waited patiently for me for forty-five years."

Conclusion

You were born to write. Forget about the lies you've been told along the way that we discussed earlier in this chapter. They have been standing in your way, but now you can forget about them. Grab your big pad of paper, and armed with your new understandings, let's move to the next chapter, where you will learn how to access, at will, the book that is dying to be released through you.

"I'm not funny. What I am is brave."

Former Sedona resident and
acclaimed actress Lucille Ball

"All of your dreams can come true if you
have the courage to pursue them."

Frequent visitor to Sedona, Walt Disney, whose
famous Thunder Mountain amusement park
ride was reportedly named after the mountain
by the same name in Sedona

chapter two

The Truth

THE ARTISTIC EXPRESSION we all seek—the one that lifts each one of us to greater heights and finally sets us free—is only accessible by turning inward, which is where all our connections with the DWW are located. But how do we access our DWW?

The Three Rs of Writing

There is a simple and exact method to access the DWW, and all it involves is following what I refer to as the Three Rs of Writing:

1. **Reserve Time to Write.** The best time to write is after a nap or a good night's sleep, at which time your left, or logical brain (which is what usually stands in your way), is still at least partially asleep or just waking up as well.
2. **Remove Distractions.** Turn off the phone and inform those to whom you are closest and/or live with when you will be writing so they won't bother you.
3. **Relax.** When you take time to relax, the interference projected by your logical mind/left brain, which I prefer to refer to as the Logical, Critical Brain—or LCB—clears, opening the way for your DWW to come streaming through your heart or Creative Connected Brain—the CCB.

The way to achieve the results you want with your writing, at all levels, is through the Three Rs of Writing. All you have to do is adhere to each of the three Rs every time you sit down to write or each time you review your writing. This is where the discipline of writing comes so strongly into play. If you take the time to follow the Three Rs of Writing each time you write or review your work, everything will go great. If you don't, your left, LCB will get in the way and your writing effort, as well as the result, will suffer miserably. Your connection with your DWW is that essential to the success of your writing. It's as simple as that.

> "A good artist should be isolated. If he isn't isolated, something is wrong."
>
> Former Sedona resident and acclaimed filmmaker and actor Orson Wells

Reserve Time to Write

Your success in this area revolves around the consistent, premeditative choosing of when it is you will attempt to write. So when do I suggest you choose to write?

I would strongly suggest that you choose to write just after waking up from a refreshing nap or a good night's sleep. Why? Because, as stated, when you have just awakened, your LCB, which tends to get in the way of any creative, heartfelt endeavor (much more on this later) is not yet awake. So doesn't it make logical sense to utilize these times to get most smoothly and easily into your writing? Of course it does.

I can both feel some of you objecting already. *"But I'm not a morning person."*

Pearl of Wisdom

All writers, especially those who are "aspiring," are already great authors of excuses. In fact, most could write volumes of excuses that explain why they have not chosen to follow the call of their writing. So if you find yourself part of this group, you are not only far from alone, but you are part of a vast majority.

Neither was I until I finally took my writing seriously. Before then, I would try to write at night, late at night, which was when I felt the calmest and most at peace—states that *are* conducive to writing effectively. However, as much as I enjoyed writing at those times, I wasn't getting the results I desired. The reason? I didn't consistently replace my bad habits with a routine that would better suit the success I craved. For example, it was rare for me to write each and every evening—I instead frequently had a social obligation, was tired, or found a movie or sports event on the tube that I "just had to see."

Once I made the switch to writing in the mornings, it all fell into place for me. My first book came streaming out of me, and all the pressures and frustrations that my lack of writing was causing—including the general dissatisfaction that I projected outward with my life and those in it—finally disappeared.

> "Courage is being scared to death but saddling up anyway."
>
> Actor and former Sedona resident John Wayne

"But [there's that word again—the one that is usually employed to confront the brilliance of any great theory or idea] *I am already getting up early."*

I was too when I first employed this simple but necessary technique. In fact, I was already getting up early after staying up late almost every night.

Please excuse me in advance for appearing callous in this regard. However, when I chose to finally and fully respond to the call of the book inside of me, I was working as a publicist with the major league baseball team the Pittsburgh Pirates. The team happened to be a great club at the time (they won the World Series during my first year on the job), which caused me to be very busy. I worked crazy hours, oftentimes during the season putting in seventeen hours a day, seven days a week, while also traveling with the team. Once you add in the hour it took me to both get ready for work and drive in each day, as you can plainly see, I had about six hours a day during which to sleep.

Just before I finally made the leap to follow the call of my writing, I was angry at seemingly everything in my life. Out of desperation (the great forefather of faith as I see it), I finally decided, at any cost, to move in the direction of my writing. Too tired to write when I got home at midnight most nights, I decided to get up two hours early each day to write before going to work.

After doing so, I regained the positive, happy me I had lost. As a result, I no longer saw everything around me as "the problem." In retrospect, I see how I owed an apology to all those who had been putting up with me at the time, for there was nothing wrong with them. Any displeasure I was feeling in my life was solely my responsibility and the result of me not doing what I was born to do. Once I started writing, I stopped projecting the dissatisfaction I felt for myself upon them.

> "It's easy to fool the mind but it's hard to fool the heart."
>
> Award-winning actor and Sedona resident Al Pacino

As you will discover for yourself, reserving a specific time to write is essential in meeting your writing/publishing goals, no matter what they are. And it is absolutely essential that you choose the best time to offer yourself the chance at success that you deserve. That's why I strongly advocate writing just after awakening from a relaxing nap or a good night's sleep.

Many times, I have worked with students on an individual basis who clearly and authoritatively state that they do their best writing at night and that is when they plan on doing it—period. I state my case, for that is what I am getting paid to do, though it usually doesn't make much of a difference because the person has already

Sedona Secret
ASK TO BE LEFT ALONE

Speak to every person or animal or whomever you are accountable to about what you will be doing and ask for their help, by leaving you alone during your chosen writing times. I cannot underrate the importance of this suggestion.

made his or her decision outside of my counsel. Not even *once* have I seen one of these people succeed. It usually takes about two to three weeks, but they cave after being unable to keep up with the quota of words I set. Then, on their own cognition, they come back to me and boldly announce that they are switching to writing in the morning, some as early as 3 or 4 A.M. Writing has won out, and shortly after that, their writing really takes off.

No, you don't have to be so anal as to write at exactly the same time each day. Again, it is not choosing the exact same time to write that will make the difference for your writing—it's choosing a specific time that would be best for your writing to break through and then doing so on a daily basis.

Pearl of *Wisdom*

There is nothing unhappier than a writer who is not writing. The main points to keep in mind about this "R" are 1) reserve time to write six days a week (more on this later as well) and 2) the best time to write is after a good night of sleep or a refreshing nap.

And, no, you do not *always* need to write first thing each and every morning. As I said, writing after having awakened from a refreshing nap works just as well. In fact, naps may become an essential part of your success as you begin to write—I'll talk much more on this later.

Remove Distractions

Even if you follow my advice and choose to write after a good night of sleep or after awakening from a nap, your mind will eventually wake up during the time when you are writing. When it does, it will attempt to distract you from writing effectively. That's why it's important to severely limit what you will be exposed to during those times, to keep yourself from being drawn away from what your writing is calling you to express.

Contrary to what most aspiring writers may believe, they are usually in supportive environments. Unfortunately, they project their dissatisfactions with themselves and their writing on those around them, which oftentimes alters their perception of this truth. As a result, they feel as if everyone around them is out to stop them from writing, when the reality is that they're holding themselves back.

The truth is that those around them don't understanding the writing bug, and don't know how to help them. As a result, they often employ counterproductive methods of "helping."

So: give these people in your life the benefit of the doubt, and assume that to one degree or another they are on your side. Second, to remove any mystery from your ambition, tell them exactly what your goals are and what you need from them to help you achieve them. Tell them that you don't need a huge homecooked breakfast or a morning pep talk—you need two uninterrupted hours each morning to write.

> "I have an everyday religion that works for me. Love yourself first, and everything else falls in line."
>
> Former Sedona resident and acclaimed actress Lucille Ball

Make your request as clear as that, and continually remind them over and over again if you have to. Soon what you are asking for will become a habit and everyone will be happier and more understanding. You'll be much happier and more fulfilled because you're writing, and they will be happier and more fulfilled because you are happy and at peace, and as result will have much more of yourself to share with them.

Yes, this even works with the blessed souls we condescendingly refer to as animals. I am fortunate to have a houseful of these unconditionally loving souls—five cats, two birds, and two dogs. The two dogs, my great dane and chow mix, love to hike each day. If it were up to them, they would hit the trail first thing each morning, which is not always possible, especially when I am in the midst of working on a book.

So in that case, I talk to them either the night before (which is most effective), or just after I get up in the morning. I remind them what I'm doing and tell them that we will be hiking in the afternoon. With their desires properly addressed, I have the calm space I need as they patiently wait for me to finish up my work.

If you find yourself in a similar situation with your pets, try my suggestion. If you take the time to speak directly from your heart, they will hear you. And being the caring, unconditional species that they are, they will respond with love.

Relax

The first two Rs are pretty easy to deal with. It's the third R, relaxing, that most people have a difficult time with because they either don't know how to relax or they try too hard to do so. As a result, many of them end up studying meditation or taking medication to relax, neither of which is necessary. Relaxing translates to quieting the mind by putting it to sleep. Simply follow these steps:

1. Sit up straight with your feet flat on the floor and your arms and legs uncrossed.
2. Close your eyes. Smile broadly for a minute or so to lighten and brighten your mood (it's nearly impossible to relax if you're not calm, and it's not possible to be calm unless you're happy).
3. Breathe deeply through your nose and exhale even more deeply through your mouth. Do this for ten consecutive breaths.

Once you are relaxed, your mind is now calm and the route to your DWW, through which all inspiration comes, is open. All you

Sedona Secret
SILENCE YOUR PHONE

Unplug or silence the phone when you are writing, in order to avoid that untimely distraction. After all, you will be responding to the callings of your DWW, the blessed author inside of you. Don't worry—if you miss a call that was really that important, someone will send the police to your home.

have to do is to give it a topic—a way to offer it a focus and/or direction (a theme or whatever—more on this later too)—and it will take off writing.

If you have a difficult time achieving your DWW connection, consider purchasing a copy of one of the subliminal CDs that I have listed on my website, *www.TomBird.com*. Any one of the three will immediately and pleasurably take you to where you want to go.

I realize that it may initially be difficult for you to consistently sit down and write. I promise all of that will change, though.

Practice What You Will Say

All you have to do is keep using the Three Rs of Writing, and in no time the positive effects of your efforts begin to take hold. You will become positively addicted to the Divine connection available to you through your writing. It's often difficult to share with other people, no matter how close you may feel to them, exactly how you feel, or what you may need from them. So let's practice doing just that before you approach your family, friends, animals, whoever, with your needs.

1. Realize that you don't have to fight or beg for what you need.
2. Remember that this is your life and you can do with it what you want.
3. The only person's permission you need to write your book is your own.
4. You will not be asking for your writing time. You will simply be stating, out of love and

Writer's
REFLECTION

Take a moment right now to recall times when you were either 1) taking a comfortable drive alone in your car; 2) on a relaxing vacation; 3) when you were comfortably alone; or 4) when you just found yourself in a really relaxed state. Make a note of a few of those times. Did you notice that during those times, you were at your creative best, as ideas just streamed through you? If so, that was the result of you relaxing and allowing your DWW to come streaming through you.

respect and as a courtesy, what you will be doing, and offering them the opportunity to participate in your heartfelt desire by helping create the space that you need. That's all.

5. Be clear about exactly what you need (two hours a day to write, six days a week). Use a large, lineless piece of paper to write that down. Make sure to be realistic and not condescending or critical of those you will be sharing this statement with, which would only serve to create an unpleasant, potentially uncooperative experience for both of you.

6. Envision each person or animal that you will be approaching. Envision one at a time. Write down what you'll be sharing with each one, and focus on how you will be sharing it.

7. After you have envisioned each case, read each description over a few times to tweak what you're sharing and the emotions and feelings you want to convey.

8. Make a firm date with yourself to talk with each individual. Thank them for hearing you out, cooperating, and loving you in this way.

the divine writer within

While I was giving a lecture at Emory University, Patty Henry, an aspiring author, repeatedly approached me during each break. Each time, she expressed the same concern: she wasn't a morning person. From what she shared, I could tell that she was a devoted mother. In fact, the only reason she got out of bed in the morning was to ready her children, who—according to her—oftentimes had to wake her up, for school. In fact, during the entire time that she and her loving husband had been together she had not been a morning person, so it had become an accepted fact in her marriage.

Finally, I tired of being asked to address the same question, over and over and over again. I looked her straight in the eye and said, "Maybe the reason you're not a morning person is because you don't have anything *you* really want to get up for." She stepped back for a moment.

"What do you mean?" she asked.

"I mean that you're always doing something for others, which is really nice of you, but what are you doing for yourself?"

> "I think it's so cool that you can pick up the guitar and create something that didn't exist five minutes ago. You can create something no one has ever heard. You have music at your fingertips."
>
> Award-winning vocalist and Sedona native Michelle Branch

I waited a moment for her to reply, which she did not take advantage of, before continuing.

"Patty, what I am saying," I said, looking her straight in the eye, "is that possibly the reason you are not a so-called 'morning person' is because you have not given yourself a good enough reason to get out of bed. Maybe making time for your beloved writing could finally be that reason," I suggested.

I had that conversation with Patty on a Saturday afternoon. The following Monday I went into my office, bright and early, and found a message Patty had left, in which she stated that she had gotten up all by herself, to write, not only Sunday but Monday as well. Patty went on to finish the first book she felt so drawn to write less than a month later.

Following the Three Rs of Writing, as it is for so many, was the key to her accomplishing her heartfelt goal.

Conclusion

The fate of your writing is totally and completely in your control. No one can stop you but yourself if you want to succeed. Success will come when you use the Three Rs of Writing each and every time you write or review your book.

Period.

chapter three

The Seventeen Principles
of Writing

ANY LACK OF success you may have experienced up to this point with writing has nothing to do with you. Why?

I'm sure whatever educational system trained you was caring and that your teachers were dedicated and hardworking, but what you were taught about how to write and what was possible for you as a writer was, in one way or another, off-base. The breakthroughs that needed to happen to better understand the art form did not transpire until a few decades ago. What you were taught had been around for potentially hundreds of years. Though the new information has been around since the 1960s, it often takes decades for new ideas and teaching methods to be integrated into our massive school systems.

The ineffective methodology you were exposed to about writing is just now, ever so slowly, starting to be replaced. This book will replace what you were taught with what you, as a writer, need to know.

Like inserting car keys into the ignition and turning over the engine, once you understand the following concepts and principles, you can immediately expect

There is nothing wrong with you as a writer, with the exception that you did what you were told and believed what had been shared with you.

massive gains, as you return to the natural, expressive ability you were born with.

The Theory of Left Brain/Right Brain

The concept of left brain/right brain is integral to your understanding of how to connect with your DWW. Roger Sperry, who won a Nobel Prize in medicine for his work, is the father of the right/left brain theory. Until Sperry's research, the medical and psychological community firmly felt that we had one brain that was divided into two identical lobes. Sperry proved this theory incorrect and established the fact that we had two identical-looking brains that were vastly different—in fact, opposites in many cases.

Left Brain/Right Brain and the Arts

Not only did Sperry's breakthrough do wonders for the work of the medical and psychological communities, it opened new doors for creative artists, who now knew where the "mystical muse" was located and, more important, how to access it. In response to Sperry's work, several critically acclaimed bestsellers were published that extended the application of the right/left brain theory into the arts.

Betty Edwards's book, *Drawing on the Right Side of the Brain*, established the fact that anyone could be artistically successful if he could get into his right brain. Edwards suggested "upside-down drawing" to transfer one's consciousness out of the controlling and oftentimes consuming left brain to the expressive right brain. Edwards told her readers to draw upside-down to confuse the left brain, which would normally get in the way of their innate artistic abilities. Drawing upside-down caused the left brain to be so confused that it just passed the images along to the right brain.

Gabrielle Rico's book, *Writing the Natural Way*, did for writers what Edwards's book did for artists. In her groundbreaking book, Rico suggests "circle drawing" or "clustering" to transfer one's consciousness from the left to the right brain. By definition, clustering or circle drawing is nothing more than a brainstorming technique designed around the random use of circles. Why circles? Simply because they are nonlinear, which means that they have no beginning and no end. As a result, the square left brain doesn't know how to interpret or use them, so it passes along whatever is inside the circles to the nondominant (at least in the Western culture) right brain. Once the information arrives in the right brain, it serves as a cue or command to draw forth out of your so-called creative side whatever you want from it. Your right brain has unlimited sources of inspiration and enlightenment and a never-forget-a-thing, long-term memory.

You'll eventually be able to harness this technique to write your book.

Relearning as Catharsis

As you retrain yourself to write in a more effective way, you'll be mimicking a similar experience oftentimes experienced in therapy, a catharsis. You're purging your old, ineffective writing instruction and replacing it with updated, successful methods. Moving through and beyond this catharsis is not only necessary to be able to effectively release the book inside you but essential to your permanently becoming the writer/author you were born to be. Even writers who are already successful don't necessarily realize they need to complete this catharsis. The full breadth of this new concept has been very slow to be accepted by and integrated into our left-brained culture.

In addition, few writers are aware that once they've completed the catharsis, their writing will take on a much less self-obsessive, pleading/resisting tone. A new tone will emerge that will be reflective of who they truly are as an author and what they are actually meant to write. Can you see now why so many first books are cathartic in nature? Writers are undergoing that transformation. This is also why so many authors of well-received or bestselling cathartic first books are unable to replicate their successes. Since none of us will live long enough to accumulate enough "emotional baggage" for a second catharsis, second books (and beyond) oftentimes lack the punch, zeal, and life of first works. The authors who don't understand the process simply continue to try to replicate the cathartic writing style of their initial works instead of pursuing the more expressive purpose and evolved literary route that is the result of being freed by their catharsis. They get stuck in the first part of the catharsis and aren't able to move past it to enjoy the fruits of their labor.

You will notice the tone and probably the direction of your writing shifting greatly after you complete the following exercises, which will move you beyond the author's catharsis we are all doomed to endure and deliver you onto the doorstep of your true, innate purpose and voice as a writer.

You Have a Decision to Make

At this time and place in your career as a writer, ask yourself:

1. Do you choose to transition *through* the catharsis by taking no more than the next six days to complete the exercises in this chapter before doing your "real writing"?
2. Would you prefer to utilize and/or sacrifice the writing of your first book to experience your catharsis?

> "A man's got to do what a man's got to do."
>
> Actor and former Sedona resident John Wayne

It's up to you. As you can probably sense from my tone, I strongly suggest transitioning through your catharsis *before* starting on your dream project. The rest of this chapter, which explains the Seventeen Principles of Writing, will help you do just that.

However, even if you choose to use your dream project as your catharsis, it is still essential for you to read over each of the following principles. You don't have to address them in the manner that I detail through the exercises, but you do have to read over them before passing on to the next section.

The Seventeen Principles of Writing

Each of these principles of writing has been designed to counteract a specific belief that has held back your development as a writer. Use your scheduled writing time for six days in the course of one week to read and complete the exercises. Then, it will be time for you to move on to the next section.

Writer's REFLECTION

Follow these steps to record how you feel about writing your book.

1. Use either the CDs you can purchase from my website or follow the Three Rs of Writing to get yourself in a DWW-connected state.
2. Position yourself in front of a stack or pad of lineless pieces of paper.
3. Write "My Book" in the center of the first piece of paper and circle it. Now release any feelings and thoughts in a rapid fire, spontaneous fashion on the paper. Quickly—don't take time to think or make sense of your reactions. Just express. As you write down each feeling or thought, circle it and connect it to the nearest circle to it before moving onto the next.
4. Keep writing and circling until you no longer experience this staccato form of expression. If you need to move to more pieces of paper, do so. Usually around the eight- to twelve-minute mark you will feel your expression begin to loosen and expand into phrases, sentences, and potentially even paragraphs. When this happens, immediately turn to another piece of paper and begin writing linearly across the paper. Stay with this form of writing until you write yourself out and have nothing to say. An example follows:

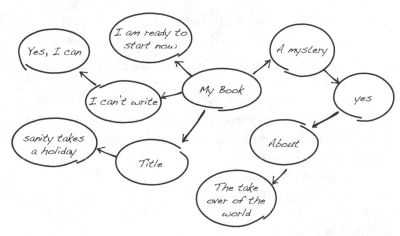

WRITING PRINCIPLE #1

The Past Does Not Determine the Future

A lot of "writing refugees" attend my classes, seminars, workshops, and retreats. By my definition, writing refugees are people who have previously, at one level or another, studied writing without having experienced the success to which they aspired. In most cases, over the years, they have used a variety of excuses to justify their lack of success: not having enough time, talent, or education; not having anything of substance anyone, including themselves, would want to read. Rarely have these refugees put the blame for their lack of success on anything or anyone outside of themselves—but that was completely opposite of the truth. The reason they had not succeeded up to this point had nothing to do with themselves, but instead with what they had been taught.

But just because you may have been taught ineffective writing tactics doesn't mean you're destined for a life of literary failure. You must commit to unlearning those ideas and learning new ones that will lead you to the success you know you can achieve. Break with your past so you can create a better future.

the divine writer within

A clinical psychologist with a PhD attended one of my classes several years ago in Virginia. I got a chance to sit down and speak with her for a few minutes before our first class together, and I was amazed at all the effort she had put into her writing up to that point without experiencing the success she desired. She had spent *years* attempting to write. She had designated a room in her home as her "writing space." She had read dozens of books on the craft and still nothing was happening for her.

After just one weekend of learning the Tom Bird Method, she was on her way to being the published author she had felt drawn to be for so long. Having gotten better in touch with her DWW in regard to what it was that she was being led to write, she took her now crystal-clear idea out to literary agents (the commissioned-based, necessary liaisons between especially new authors and book publishers). In no time at all, dozens of agents had expressed interest in the representation of her book, which she hadn't even written yet. After aligning herself with the agent who was the best match, her representative sold her book in about three weeks.

This same person continued writing and has since published several more books. If she, like so many thousands of others in her situation, had not believed in Principle #1: The Past Does Not Determine the Future, she would never have been open to doing something different than she had been doing up to that point. As a result, she would never have come to my classes, learned a different route, and gone on to the success she has since enjoyed.

WRITING PRINCIPLE #2

You Alone Are Responsible for Creating Your Own Successes

I alluded to this earlier, but let me clarify. The world is full of people who are just not ready. You know the ones I mean—those who are continually making excuses why they are not doing this or that, and who continually, in one way or another, sabotage their own efforts. Maybe you were there before you picked up this book. Maybe the reason you picked up this book was because you were ready to finally take responsibility for your own success.

Writer's
REFLECTION
Take a moment to ponder the situation and feelings you were experiencing before you picked up this book. What led you to read it? The encouragement or complaining of those closest to you? Your own pain and dissatisfaction with at least this area of your life? Other signs that may have popped up?

I know that I wasn't ready to accept that responsibility until I finally had the conversation with God, which I mentioned in the Introduction. After that, I was ready. I guess you could say that the desperation I was experiencing was the forefather of my readiness. Based upon my own experiences and those of my students, I have come to see the true importance and necessity of desperation.

Desperation is the forefather of faith.

Whatever got you to this point has changed you. You are finally ready to create your own success. You are no longer allowing the past to determine your future and you are taking responsibility for your own success.

The methods in this book will lead you to the success you desire. It really is that simple I attest to this through my own success, and I can also point to tens of thousands of my students who have gone on to write and publish books. There is no longer anything standing in your way.

Pearl of *Wisdom*

So much about life is just showing up. Many people show up physically for work or for life, but does every part of them show up? No. In most cases, their body may be there, but their heart, desire, and mind are not. Every part of you needs to show up for your writing.

Because so few people do so, all you have to do to succeed in this life is to show up—all of you—your heart, your soul, your attention, your desire—YOU!

You are taking responsibility for creating your own success by showing up and, as a result, you can expect your results to change dramatically in the near future.

Even the publishing industry is not standing in your way. As I illustrate later in Chapter 8, it often doesn't matter to those in the industry whether you have a degree or not, or what your age or color or socioeconomic background is. If you have a passion for something that you want to communicate in writing and are both familiar with and employ the correct etiquette, you will find that a strong percentage of agents are more than happy to represent your book or that a strong percentage of publishers are more than happy to work directly with you.

the divine writer
within

Myra was a student of mine who attended one of my weekend classes in Knoxville. A very driven writer, Myra had been faithfully attending a monthly writer's group in her local area, yet had gone absolutely nowhere with getting her book written and/or published.

I told Myra that she needed to unlearn some bad habits and take responsibility for her own success. Excited, she couldn't wait to share my thoughts with the members of her writing group. Much to her surprise, though, the information was met with a staunch rejection she never expected.

Why? Misery loves company. Those in Myra's writers' group had always used one excuse or another to justify their lack of writing success. Not every writers' group is like this, of course, but Myra's happened to be. Never once had they looked at themselves as the potential cause of their failure and, as a result, when Myra offered them the solutions that they were supposedly open to, they rejected everything she had to share.

Myra left the group shortly afterward. She was no longer willing to be a part of a group that would not take responsibility for their own success or, in this case, was so communally frightened of succeeding that they took turns sabotaging each other's efforts.

When Myra left the group, she took back control of her life, put into play what she had learned in my class, and finished her first book less than a month later. *Myra took responsibility for creating her own success.*

WRITING PRINCIPLE #3

Writing Can Be Fast, Easy, and Fun

No matter what task you're trying to do, it will always be more difficult or downright unsuccessful if you approach it incorrectly. Is writing difficult for you in any way? I'm guessing it is. That's because you've been going about it the wrong way.

That's right, you've been doing things wrong. Is that your fault? No. You were just taught incorrectly. How could that be the case? Billions are spent on our educations and the training of our teachers and professors each year. Do I mean to say that the money devoted to writing has been squandered on incorrect philosophies and approaches? Yes.

Just think about it for a minute. If you are enrolled in a college class on nursing, let's say, there's an excellent chance that the professor teaching the course is a proven, certified nurse. The same goes for other areas such as law, accounting, psychology, education, business, and any of the sciences.

However, what do you get when you take a college course on writing? Is the person a proven author, a successful writer? Probably not. Since they are not really qualified to teach you something that they have not yet accomplished, neither are they capable of distinguishing between right and wrong methods. And who designed the writing curriculum for these teachers? You guessed it—people just as unqualified.

These teachers probably gave you in-depth instructions on how to follow exactly in their footsteps. And if you follow their path, where will it lead you? To the same lack of success that they themselves experienced. Is it any wonder, then, that you are where you are as a writer? Is it any wonder that writing has been so darn hard and painful for you?

However, it's not *their* fault that they shared with you what they did. They were doing the best they could and they didn't know any better. You see, because so few people really understand the craft of writing—even though it's been around for centuries—no one taught it properly until some necessary breakthroughs transpired in the late 1960s. And it takes quite a long time to integrate new ideas into our educational systems.

Forget your unqualified teachers. Let's approach this subject from a more positive perspective. I am assuming that there were times when your writing just seemed to flow out of you. You felt the flow, you know it exists, and it feels so darn good. You just don't know how to get to it consistently.

My old buddy Jack, who's an avid golfer, has always encouraged me to try it out. I always refuse, and Jack counters by saying something like, "If I could get you out on the course and just once, even it if was by accident, you hit the ball just right and heard that magical 'ping,' you'd be hooked for life." I know that to be the case, of course, which is why I haven't taken up the game. I consider myself too busy with other things to become "hooked for life" on golf.

I know this situation well, as do you. For I have seen tens of thousands of people enter into my classes, who were hooked to their writing for life.

When you are hooked on your writing and can regularly find your ping, you'll also find your speed (which will begin to moderate itself as you begin to write consistently). The ability to write quickly comprises not only the foundation of your DWW expression (which is initially trying to outrun the constraints of your left brain), but is the basis of the two-draft concept that I'll discuss later.

When you are one with the ping of your DWW, you will not only be writing well, but enjoying it and succeeding at it too! That's where the fun comes in.

Sedona Secret
SILENCE YOUR PHONE

Those of you who have heard, experienced, and felt the "ping" of writing, know exactly what has kept you coming back to it for so long. Now all you have to do is to learn how to find that ping every time you approach your writing. Hearing that ping also helps you write faster—you know, when the words spurt out of you faster than you can write them down.

WRITING PRINCIPLE #4

All the Inspiration You Will Ever Need Is Already Inside You

Let me say this up front: I apologize for any shock or disappointment that the following statements may cause:

1 There is no Easter Bunny (Santa Claus, I'm still not too sure about).
2. There is no such thing as the Muse—the mystical, magical being and/or essence that supposedly visits artists from the outside whenever it wants, and if it ever wants.

For centuries, the Muse has caused artists endless hours of frustration and madness—but has also supplied its share of exhilaration. When the Muse visited, all went well: masterpieces were painted on the ceilings of famous chapels, classic novels were written, and majestic sculptures were formed. When the Muse was absent, however, artists spiraled into drunkenness, dereliction, depression, madness, and even suicide. These supposedly powerless but passionate artists wondered what they had to do, where they had to be, or what they had to say to once again lure the Muse back into their lives.

Our culture is so obsessed with the Muse that a movie called *The Muse* was actually produced on the topic, featuring the award-winning actress Sharon Stone. In the movie, all who visited Stone (the Muse), received magical, creative, expressive powers, much like what the artists of the past believed. When they were out of her favor, however, all they had been given disappeared and they slumped greatly, not only as artists but personally as well. With this belief so firmly rooted in culture and in so many celebrated writers—from Kerouac to Wolfe to Hemingway—is it any wonder that people want to find their Muse?

Here's a secret. The brilliance that this alleged Muse provides is actually available to every person, no matter what his or her station in life. If you choose to believe in the Muse—or decide use her as your excuse to keep you from doing what your heart calls you to do—you're relinquishing responsibility for your success to her. And that's in direct conflict with Principle #2!

Pearl of *Wisdom*

The truth is that access to the inspiration you're seeking is inside you, which is why you have never been able to outrun or ignore it no matter how hard you tried. It was always right there, all the time, inside you.

The Creative Connected Brain

The base of the inspiration that lives inside you is mentally housed in what I refer to as your Creative, Connected Brain (**CCB**—which is oftentimes, as well, seen as the right or connected brain), whose primary purpose is to release your Divine Writer Within's purpose or message in an unconditional, passionate way.

If your creative brain has the power to express your amazing gifts, what has kept your writing from flowing freely at all times? The influence of your **LCB**, or logical, critical brain—your other, more logic-based side.

Your LCB versus Your CCB

You see, there couldn't be two more complete opposites than your LCB and CCB.

1. The LCB's primary purpose is to avoid pain. Your CCB's primary purpose is to express the results of your heartfelt connection with the Divine Writer Within.
2. The LCB communicates through thinking, analyzing, and criticizing, while the CCB communicates through feelings.
3. The LCB is conditional. It always comes from one perspective and one perspective only: will whatever it is that you are about to partake in cause you pain? If so, it will avoid it at all costs. On the other hand, the CCB is unconditional by nature. It's always honest and heartfelt. It feels, it expresses, it doesn't

worry about repercussions, and why should it, since it never comes from a place of malice?

4. The LCB has very limited capabilities. In fact, when you were born, your LCB was like a blank hard drive. It knew absolutely nothing. And everything it learned from that point forward came from conditioning: rote and repetition associated with your five senses.

   On the other hand, your CCB has unlimited capabilities because it draws from the much higher perspective of a direct connection with your Divine Writer Within. You've probably already experienced the thrill of a few gems of brilliance that came flowing through your writing, but you may not have known where they came from. Well, now you know—your CCB's direct connection with the DWW.

5. The LCB houses your short-term memory, whose lone connection to the world is that which enters into it consciously through the five senses. This skeletal interpretation is housed for a short period of time before being released. If you live in your LCB most of the time, this short-term information recall is why you may not remember where you left your car keys.

   Conversely, the CCB draws from a much deeper connection to life than the five senses and has memory storage capabilities far greater than the LCB's. That's why, while living in your CCB, you are able to recall, with great richness and feeling, incidents that transpired years, if not decades, before.

   The CCB draws from its long-term memory to access the depth, color, feeling, analogy, and, most of all, the universality needed to touch hearts, including your own. You may find that your writing sometimes expresses these memories.

6. The LCB sleeps while the CCB doesn't. Have you ever awakened in the middle of the night and needed to write? Have you ever been driving along in your car and, suddenly, out of nowhere, your mind was overwhelmed by an inspiration? How about when you were relaxing on vacation and this same type of inspiration hits you? What do all these occurrences have in

common? In each and every case, your LCB had been asleep or unguarded, allowing your connection with your CCB to finally come streaming through.

Why do you have to be almost "out of it" before you are able to connect with this obviously powerful CCB? The answer to that question is simple but far reaching.

The Characteristics of Your LCB Versus Your CCB

Your LCB	Your CCB
Purpose: Avoid pain	Purpose: Expression
Thinks, evaluates, criticizes	Feels
Conditional	Unconditional
Limited capabilities	Unlimited capabilities
Short-term memory	Long-term memory
Sleeps	Never sleeps
Falsely dominant	Innately dominant

How Your Logical Brain Tries to Protect You

When you were born, you maintained a natural, direct connection to your DWW through your CCB. Think about babies' behavior—it's free-flowing, expressive, heartfelt, unconditional, and spontaneous. At a certain point, however (often around age two), being so open and expressive led to pain (which might have come in the form of scolding or punishment). Until then, you had probably been pretty well unconditionally accepted. But by the time you were two, you had learned to speak and speak you did—maybe too often, too loudly, too openly, and too honestly.

> "The chaperone's job is to make sure that no one else has any fun."
>
> Actress and Sedona resident
> Jane Russell

The fact is that your parents, your family, and your town or city were living in an unnatural LCB world, and they had begun to share it with you. Yet they were just afraid. They didn't want you to be subjected to the same pain they had been exposed to—the pain of criticism, rejection of their true selves, and scolding and punishment. At other times, their fears took the form of a destroy-at-all-costs envy.

As a result, your LCB began to associate the deep connection you feel with your writing (which is free flowing, expressive, heartfelt, and so on) with the same part of you that was not accepted as a child (since those were also characteristics of your unacceptable behavior as a child). Thus, your LCB does everything possible to keep you from associating with your DWW connection, which is why it has fought to keep you from writing the way you want to write. This is also why it may have ruthlessly judged/criticized whatever you did write. It just didn't want you to be hurt through the sharing of your writing with anyone else, as you were hurt when you shared the same behaviors with your parents. That's all. So in this way, your LCB has been a very good friend. However, all the actions it has taken in regard to your writing have been counterproductive.

WRITING PRINCIPLE #5

You Can Access a Connection to Your Unlimited Expression at Any Time

How can you access your Divine Writer Within? Through the Three Rs of Writing. How can you continue to deepen and strengthen this most exciting of all connections? By continuing to use the Three Rs on a regular basis, until finding and living through this connection becomes as natural and routine as breathing. That's how easy it was meant to be.

RETRAIN YOUR LCB

To reverse all that your LCB has learned, and to get it on your side—as it has been in so many other successful endeavors in your life—all we have to do is retrain it, which is one of the major focuses of this book.

WRITING PRINCIPLE #6

You Have a Very Special Message to Share Through Your Writing

My teaching has exposed me to people of different backgrounds, ages, beliefs, and life experiences, and I've found that *every* person has a very special message to share.

Instead of wondering whether writing in a particular style or genre is "good enough," ask yourself: "Did I open myself up to that unique, unconditional love and acceptance offered by my DWW? Did I share that very special message through my writing?"

Simply by dedicating yourself to being a more effective writer, I believe you can answer "yes." Again: *It is not the form your writing takes that determines its significance as much as how it affects, and if it does affect, the lives, minds, and—mostly—the hearts of those who read it.*

Pearl of *Wisdom*

It really doesn't matter what you write or what form your writing takes—nonfiction, a Western, poetry. As long as it springs forth from your DWW, it will not only be good—it will be exactly what your DWW was attempting to express through you. Even if the book that came streaming through you ended up being a light romance, it is still a work of significance if it made people smile, laugh, cry, or feel, and, in doing so, touched their hearts.

WRITING PRINCIPLE #7

Fast Writing Is Always the Best Writing

I can guarantee you that every bit of writing that has ever positively influenced your life, mood, or day was written by someone in a Divine Writer Within–connected state. I can also guarantee you that while this person was in this state, he or she was writing fast. Yes, fast.

Writing is an art of the heart, not of the head. That doesn't mean that all the writing you have been exposed to has come from the heart. In fact, much of the writing you have been exposed to—real estate contracts, insurance forms, etc.—have come from the LCB. But have you sought out these writings for inspiration, guidance, or enlightenment? Has what you have read in these documents made you feel deeply about something that could be considered positive? Have they positively changed your day, your mood, your life? I think not.

> Pearl of *Wisdom*
>
> Writing fast is essential because the faster you write, the less time you have to think.

Clearly, you *can* write out of the LCB. It is difficult, time-consuming, unfulfilling, at times painful, and it doesn't usually lead to any positive, inspiring result for the reader—but you can do it. But you probably want to inspire your reader in some way, right? You don't want to settle for LCB writing, you want CCB writing. To get out of your LCB and into your CCB, you need to write fast.

How Fast Should I Write?

My experience has shown that your DWW will typically express through your CCB at a rate of 1,200 to 2,400 words per hour, with an average writing speed of 1,500 words per hour.

What does it mean if you write slower than that speed? It means that your writing and your writing experience will be held back by inappropriate LCB-based intervention. What then does that translate to? A lousy, frustrating, unfinished experience.

Imagine you have a brand new, shiny car, the exact model and style you always wanted. You have the keys in your hand. Your problem? The car is in a garage, with the door closed. You can see your car through the windows at the top of the garage door, which makes this entire experience that much more frustrating—you can see the car, in all its beauty, but you can't get to it.

Of course, the car in this analogy represents the book inside of you, which is trying to get out. The garage door represents your LCB. To get to your car and drive it out of the garage, you have to lift up the garage door—not partially, but *all* the way up.

If you are trying to write with the garage door only halfway or three-quarters of the way up, that's not enough. You have to lift that garage door all the way up to get the entire car all the way out. Then, and only then, will you feel the peace of accomplishment and full-hearted expression your soul longs for. If you're writing at a speed below an average of 1,200 words an hour, your garage door is only partway up. You're experiencing inappropriate LCB-based interference, which could lead to a wide range of problems. Remember, your LCB still believes that writing and the sharing of it is a painful thing. So it will do anything it can to try to keep you from it, or to create a self-fulfilling prophecy of failure. It is still too early in the process to expect a lifetime worth of bad training to be erased—it will take the writing of your book to do that. Until then, it is very important that you keep an eye sharply tuned to your writing speed so you can gauge your LCB's influence. How do you do that? By counting words.

Exercise: Counting Words

Once you get to this point in the process, you'll need to start tracking how fast you're writing. For your next few writing sessions, count the number of words you wrote and divide it by the amount of time you wrote. How do you do that? Pick out an average-looking line from what you wrote (not an average-looking sentence). Count the number of words in that line and write it down. Now count the number of lines you wrote in your session and write that down. Multiply those two numbers. That will equal the average number of words you wrote in the session.

To come up with the number of words per hour you averaged while writing in this session, divide your total number of words by the number of hours you wrote. For example, if you wrote 1,500 words in one hour, divide 1,500 by one for a total of 1,500. If you wrote 1,500 words in forty-five minutes (or three quarters of an hour), divide your total by .75, which would equal a writing speed of 2,000 words per hour.

Again, remaining at a speed of at least 1,200 words an hour, the low-water mark, is essential to avoid any unnecessary, oftentimes subliminal hassles of inappropriate LCB intervention.

Tips for Writing Faster

What if your writing speed falls below 1,200 words per hour? There are several things you can immediately consider:

1. **Have you been following the Three Rs of Writing faithfully?** If not, this could be the source of your problems, especially if you have not been focusing deeply enough on relaxing. If that is the case, use the CDs listed on my website, *www.TomBird.com*.
2. **How is your pen working?** Yes, I said "pen." A pencil or a fine- or felt-tipped pen will substantially slow down your writing speed because they have a tendency to grab onto the fibers of your paper much more than a ballpoint or gel pen. If you need to, this is the time to test-drive a new pen or two before continuing.
3. **Are you experiencing a significant amount of pain in your hand or wrist when you are writing?** Pain like this can come from two sources. First, it might be the result of an LCB-CCB battle, which manifests at the back of your neck and makes its way down your arm through the tightening of tendons and muscles. Second, it might indicate a structural problem in your wrist or hands, in which case writing in longhand for any length of time may be too much for you. (For example, carpal tunnel is one example of a structural problem, but there are others as well.) In that case, I start out by writing in longhand for, say, fifteen minutes before switching over to writing on a keyboard. Then, approximately every fifteen minutes, switch back to writing on paper just to ensure you are continually in the necessary CCB-based state throughout your writing session.

4. **Try taking it 300 words at a time.** If none of the first three ideas make a difference, mark off sections on your writing surface equivalent to the amount of space you would need to write 300 words. Then keep track of the time you are writing and work to write to the end of each 300-word section by the time fifteen minutes passes. As simple as this exercise may sound, it's very effective, and I have seen it do more than anything else to quickly bring up the writing speed to an acceptable level.

Once you begin writing at the rate of at least 1,200 words per hour, you will feel a shift, a difference—that's the result of inappropriate LCB intervention falling to the wayside.

Pearl of *Wisdom*

Ninety-five percent of the mistakes you could make as a writer are the result of inappropriate LCB intervention. I'm talking about errors that tie directly into the LCB's ability to move you away from your flow and the voice of your DWW. If that happens, you're likely to overthink, judge, criticize your own work, and thus to lose your direct, heartfelt connection with the reader. Your enhanced writing speed is essential because when you are writing fast, you don't have time to think. Also, when you're connected to your DWW through your CCB, your writing will be at its best.

WRITING PRINCIPLE #8

You Can Complete a Book in Three to Five Weeks by Writing Two Hours a Day, Six Days a Week

Do the math. Two hours a day, writing at the pace of 1,500 words per hour, equals 3,000 words per writing session. Six days a week at this pace equals 18,000 words per week. At that rate, how long would it take you to write a 60,000-word book, which is somewhere near the average length of an adult American book? Yeah, you get where I'm coming from.

"But wait," you say, "no one writes a book that fast!"

Well, Jack Kerouac used to write a book in three or four days, during which time he was continually connected to what he thought to be the Muse. There goes that theory.

"Okay, okay," you say, "but if you write a book in that short a period of time, it's gonna be crap."

If we were talking about aging wine or cheese in that short of a period of time, I would have to agree with you. But we're talking about writing, which, because of all the reasons I stated in the previous principle, is best done fast. In fact, the slower you write, the more inappropriate LCB interference you'll encounter. And you'll find *more* writing errors when you work at a slow writing speed, because of the LCB's influence.

WRITING PRINCIPLE #9

Writing on Large, Lineless Pieces of Paper Offers Your DWW the Surface It Craves to Be Able to Passionately Express Itself

As I said, 95 percent of the mistakes you could make with your writing are automatically cured by doing away with inappropriate LCB-based intervention. The other 5 percent are eliminated by writing on large, lineless pieces of paper. Why?

1. The blank pieces of paper, obviously void of lines and margins, are more conducive to the expressions of the unconditional, unlimited attributes of your DWW.
2. Writing on large, lineless pieces of paper offers a writer the perspective necessary to see where he or she has been or is going at all times. Because the width of the lines is so narrow, it's impossible to see, at a quick glance, much of what you have written. If you are able to keep track of your progress, you're less likely to run into a writer's biggest technical problem: redundancy.

The Ongoing Benefits of Using Lineless Paper

Am I saying that you have to write in longhand on large, lineless pieces of paper for the rest of your life? Even though that would probably be a great idea, I realize that, even though they offer a tremendous amount of convenience for your DWW, they are inconvenient on another end—you still have to type your work so you can submit it electronically to a publisher. Try using the lineless paper for at least one book, if not two. By that time, your atrophied CCB will probably have gained enough strength to stand up to your at-times challenging LCB, allowing you to express your CCB in a more structured format (say, a computer).

I'm just proactive. Why do more drafts and make writing any harder than it needs to be by letting your LCB influence your writing more than it should?

Think Like a Kid

I know, I've already given you plenty of reasons to write on lineless paper. But here's one more. Why do you think kids, who are still living through their CCBs, want to write on walls? Are they not the biggest, lineless, most unconditional spaces in the house? When kids want to draw and write through their CCBs, they intuitively find large, lineless "paper." So for you to be able to express your CCB's message completely and successfully, try taking your kids' lead.

Would you be surprised to hear that William Faulkner, an author ahead of his time, wrote on the walls of his house? Or that internationally recognized genius Walt Disney did all his plotting and planning on large lineless sheets of paper? You're in good company.

Sedona Secret
USE LINELESS PAPER

When you write quickly from a DWW-connected state on large, pieces of lineless paper for two hours at a time, you'll find that you finish your book in no time. Not only will this technique minimize the mistakes, but you will end up with a "finished" rough draft. You'll find that your writing is already infused with the depth, direction, passion, and heart that most authors, even world-famous ones, often need several drafts to achieve.

WRITING PRINCIPLE #10

You Are Doing Your Best Writing When You Don't Know Where You Are Going

I know, you're wondering how you can possible write unless you've got your entire book planned out, perhaps to the last detail. Nope. Let's think about it. The part of you that is conditional and thus needs to know where your writing is going is your logical brain. But, if you are maintaining your writing speed at such a level that you are outrunning any LCB-based intervention, your LCB will not *know where you are going.*

You have to get out of that LCB mindset that tells you that you need a well-thought-out plan. Your CCB should be running the show. Think of it like this: In essence, the experience of *writing* a book very much mirrors that of *reading* one. If you know by page fourteen exactly what the author is going to share and how the book is going to end, would you continue to read it? Probably not. Your DWW, as it streams through your CCB, knows this and uses it to your advantage. How? If, in the same vein, you sat down to write a book and knew exactly how each detail of it was going to be laid out all the way through to the end, would you have the same zest for writing it? Probably not. So *not* knowing where you're going is a *good* thing because it coaxes you through to the completion of a project and helps you maintain excitement and motivation. Don't worry. Not knowing where you are going really is a *good* thing. When I tell students to try writing this method, however, they're always skeptical. I tell them to just keep writing and not read the whole thing until it's finished. When it's time to read what they've written, they say something like, *"I'm sure it's going to suck. I mean, I don't even know what I wrote about!"*

Sedona Secret
LESS IS MORE

The less of an understanding of a topic you have while writing a book + less LCB intervention = a better book.

Much to their delight, they all come away pleasantly surprised with their result after reading their works for the first time. These positive results can be attributed to Principle #10.

> **Pearl of** *Wisdom*
>
> When writing your book, your priorities will shift substantially from writing for a *result* to writing for the *process*. You will be motivated less by wanting to get the book done and more by your desire to come back to the pen and paper over and over and over again to get that rush of excitement your DWW provides. You will no longer struggle with caring where the story is going or with which character is doing what—and remember, that's a good thing.

Archetypes

Part of the success of Principle #10 comes directly as a result of connecting with your archetypes. From a literary standpoint, I define archetypes as *"symbolic representations of universal meanings."* And what does *that* mean?

- If you're writing fiction, your archetypes are your characters.
- If you're writing nonfiction, your archetypes will be embodied in the essence of the themes, theories, and/or voice or tone that make up your book.

Yes, they literally push along the pen in your hand, where they want it to go, writing whatever they want you to write. They know where your writing is going, even when you and your LCB don't. At their deepest level, archetypes deliver your personal message. They tell you to write whatever your DWW is composing for you. Clearly, they're important influences! That's why you need to fully discover and understand your personal archetypes before you can successfully convey your DWW's message.

Even though succumbing to this divine connection can make you feel so much less important than your ego wants you to feel, it's a whole lot easier to write what your archetypes want you to write. You're probably still a little confused. Let me clarify the two types of archetypes so that your LCB can better understand this experience, and not interrupt your writing process trying to figure it out.

THE TRANSITIONAL ARCHETYPE

In most cases, the first type of archetype to surface is the Transitional Archetype (TA). These archetypes are produced by the CCB and exist for one purpose only: to help you remove whatever biases may exist (most of which are against you and/or your abilities) so that you can move along with your writing. TAs typically appear in your mind as an image of someone you love and trust, and rarely, if ever (unless you are writing an autobiographical book), end up being a part of your book. You'll know when a TA is making an appearance in your writing, because you will react very strongly on a personal level once he or she (or the theme or tone) appears.

When I lead an exercise designed to release TAs as part of one of my lectures, it is not unusual for students to become very emotional. Some start crying; some become angry; others are soulfully touched as the result of an understanding or enlightenment their TAs share with them. Regardless of the type of reaction they have, the students are always concerned that these very personal experiences might become a part of (or even the focus of) their book. I tell them that these TAs are helping them release any bias they may have—most of which are against themselves—that could keep them from writing to the best of their abilities. Once I confirm who the archetype is and what he or she actually represents, writers usually quickly get back into the flow of their writing, armed with their new understandings and confidence. They can move rapidly through whatever the TAs have to share with them.

Who are some of the typical TAs to appear through my students' work?

> "I put myself into character for my songs."
>
> Award-winning vocalist and Sedona native
> Michelle Branch

- The CCB often uses **grandparents**, or images of grandparents, to convey understandings, messages, and appreciations. Oftentimes, especially in today's world when both parents work and are busy, grandparents provide a great deal of their grandchildren's spiritual nurturing. And since writing (when done from the essential core) deals with the spirit, who better to deliver a spiritual message than a grandparent? After all, that person has probably already effectively communicated to the heart of the writer.

- Present **spouses** oftentimes appear for the same reason. If a writer has been married more than once, it's the true love (thus, usually not the first spouse) that emerges.

- **Former lovers** from the distant past, oftentimes first lovers, appear quite frequently as well. They usually represent a more innocent and true time in a writer's life, which is why all of sudden they become so valuable. Remember, a big part of the author's transformation is to reclaim his or her CCB, which prevailed (or was at least more in control) in his or her younger days.

- **First- and last-born children** show up frequently as TAs. It's especially common if the writer had children at a young age—say, twenty. At times, that child actually helps the young parent grow up. They show up during the writing process because they may serve as a confidante and/or teacher in the life of the writer. The youngest appears because they are often the ones adored the most and thus the one to whom the writer feels the closest.

- **New friends** with whom a writer has formed a rapid but close relationship appear regularly. This person usually reflects the writer's progress in his or her self-acceptance, especially if the writer had a significant awakening in this area. Because people tend to attract friends who mirror their own personalities, these new friends probably reflect the writer's newfound self-awareness. Thus, these new friends often appear because they are similar in personality to the person inside the writer who they have come to love.

- **Jesus Christ, or some other religious reflection**, shows up regularly as well, especially if the writer maintains a deep spiritual or religious connection.

For example, perhaps you're working on a novel and begin writing about a character's next-door neighbor, a kindly old WWII veteran who plays checkers. You quickly realize that you're describing your own grandfather. That's a TA. Or, say you're writing about birds and you realize that the language you're using to describe their mating calls also describes your relationship with your first love. That's a TA.

No matter who appears and in what form, your TA is showing up for a specific reason. That reason may not have anything directly to do with the actual writing of your book, but it does have to do with helping you eliminate biases and/or emotions that are holding you back as a writer. It is absolutely essential for you to keep in mind that at its core, writing is a very deep and personal art form expressed most effectively through passion or emotion. Oftentimes the emotion that's released may deal with something you don't want to face for one reason or another. That is where the TA comes in. Whoever appears as a TA will help you understand and deal with these raw emotions. If you don't clear away this emotional baggage, there is absolutely no way to spread the next archetype's (the Primary Archetype) message. The TA ensures that you are emotionally ready for the PA.

THE PRIMARY ARCHETYPE

Once the TAs' job is done—poof!—they're gone, never to be seen in this form again. They make way for the second type of archetype, the Primary Archetype (PA). This person may show up as someone you have never seen before, someone much older or younger than you, as the type of person you detest or mistrust, or as someone very alluring. Either way, he or she will be someone you have very strong feelings in response to (either negative or positive) and someone you will need to get to know much, much better to understand why you feel as you do.

PAs deliver the messages found at the heart of your writing, yet they often represent the unknown. As a result, PAs are normally personified by individuals you have never seen or to whom you have never been introduced, and they may represent a place you've never been or an experience you've never had. As you can imagine, PAs are most prevalent in the writing of fiction, since they most prevalently appear as characters in novels.

Since your LCB equates familiarity with safety, you must introduce your PAs to your LCB. That way, your LCB will not try to deny your PA's existence and thus smother the story your PA is trying to help you tell.

EXERCISE: GET TO KNOW YOUR PA

To get to know your PAs at a level that will allow your LCB to accept them, ask any PAs that appear the following questions and write down their responses, as they move through your mind, onto your pieces of lineless paper. Here are the questions:

1. If you were a road, where would you lead and why? (The "why" part of this and the following questions are the most important part because the answering of them forces the PA into sharing a much greater, necessary insight into him or her. This insight will enable him or her to take on the necessary feel and form to be effective.) Let me explain further. The PA is like the seed from which the plant (your storyline) appears. However, if you refuse to understand and thus be able to trust the PA, the storyline will either have to struggle to appear or you will stop the storyline from being released at all. Trusting the PA is the

Sedona Secret
JOIN A WRITER'S GROUP?

Many students ask me if writing groups are beneficial. The answer is: they are, in a select few cases. Find a group that is headed by a successful, knowledgeable, and egoless published writer with a proven system to share. If you can do so, you will probably have found a fertile place to learn, grow, and succeed. To make it easier on yourself, join my online community of authors at *www.TomBird.com*, and I will hook you up with a list of already established writing groups in your area you can join. I even list others across the country that you can visit when in their locales.

key to releasing not only the full essence of PAs, but also the full depth of the storylines they will release to you. Thus, you need to get to know the PAs so you can build the necessary trust and the rest of your book can evolve.

2. If you were a fish, animal, or fowl, what would you be? Why?
3. What one event or circumstance in your life did more to make you into who you are than any other and why?

Please note that if you answer these questions quickly and easily, you are probably not allowing yourself to go to the depth that is absolutely necessary.

The answering of each question by a PA usually takes several pages, especially if the PA is a main character. The only way to determine without a shadow of a doubt if a PA is a main or secondary character is to ask each one the above three questions. You may experience several PAs, some of whom are more important (main) than others (secondary). The secondary characters will not go into much depth in their replies, while the main ones will go on for what may seem like forever. This depth allows your LCB to get enough information on them and their backgrounds to trust them to do their work.

With all of this explanation, your LCB should now be able to differentiate between TAs and PAs, so that it can accept that *they* know where your writing is going when it doesn't.

WRITING PRINCIPLE #11

Don't Read What You Have Written Until You Have Completed Your Book

Yeah, what I am saying is to refrain from reading your writing until you have completely finished it. Why?

1. **Reading your material brings forth your LCB, and you want to keep your writing as far away from it as possible.** If you stop to read any portion of your material during the writing process, you

actually stop *or slow your progress*. As we've discussed, writing *faster* helps maintain your connection to your DWW. *So if you stop the flow of your DWW through the CCB and bring out the LCB, you've only succeeded in bringing your writing to a halt. And that'd be awfully frustrating.*

2. **You'll protect your CCB.** Wait until your CCB has gained considerable strength through the writing of your book and can stand up to what may be the previously unmatched strength of your LCB. If you allow your LCB to judge your writing harshly—and potentially unfairly—before your CCB has regained control of your writing, all you've done is destroy whatever progress your CCB has made thus far.

WRITING PRINCIPLE #12

Hold All Research to the End of Your Book

In the same vein as Principle #11, stopping to research facts, figures, dates, descriptions, and so on during the writing process interrupts the flow of your DWW through your CCB. And with each interruption your CCB stands a chance of being shut down for good. Making time to research while writing simply isn't worth the risk.

Pearl of *Wisdom*

My experience has shown that more than 90 percent of the information collected before the writing of a book (from here on referred to as prewriting research) does not end up surfacing in the final draft of the book. In essence then, *prewriting research equates to socially accepted procrastination.*

Yes, I know. You've heard many authors claim they had researched for dozens of years before finally sitting down to write their books. But that doesn't mean that they couldn't have written the same book much, much faster—and possibly even *better*—if they had shared my belief that there was an already-written book inside of them just trying to get out. If they had believed that idea, they would probably have worked in a similar fashion to the method I have been employing and sharing with my students for so long. They would have simply written whatever book that they felt coming out of them, simply noting gaps in their understanding of facts, figures, names, dates, descriptions, or whatever. Then they'd return to address those gaps at a later time through what I refer to as postwriting research.

I'm sure that you can see how this approach to research can significantly shorten the writing time of any book from taking several years to just a few months, if unnecessary prewriting research is eliminated all together. You're not wasting your time on research you don't need to do, and can focus on only the information your writing needs after it's finished.

A lot of students ask me something like, *"But what happens if I'm writing a book based on interviews or something like that?"* Good question. In all cases, release whatever book is in you. Let it show you what it is and what it needs. In some cases, you will find that a book needs the addition, through postwriting research, of a few dates, names, and figures. Others will need some developed description. Others, such as a book of interviews, will come out in a skeletal fashion, offering not much more than an introduction and a developed outline. In any case, when you go back to do your postwriting research, no matter how skimpy or substantial it may be, you will know exactly what you're looking for. The process will not take any longer than absolutely necessary, and your final version will comprise, on all levels, your finest effort possible. Period.

Sedona Secret
DON'T DRAG IT OUT

Myriad problems arise if an author spends too long writing one project. Remember: *Your most valuable asset is your own voice expressed in a passionate, heartfelt manner.* Even the slowest-growing person changes substantially over a long period of time, which means that his or her voice alters too. So if it takes you a long time to write your book, you can bet that several different, potentially conflicting voices will be present in your finished version. In addition, writing fast at all times keeps your LCB in its place.

WRITING PRINCIPLE #13

All Great and Effective Writing Is the Result of a Direct Interaction with Your DWW

Some of my students over the years have thought that I only taught my methods to help writers with so-called "creative" projects, such as writing fiction. In every case, what they didn't understand was that *all writing projects are potentially "creative" and that the job of writing is to communicate effectively no matter what the genre.*

Now some people who write fail miserably at this, of course. For example, take the people who, as mentioned earlier, write the majority of contracts, insurance agreements, and the like. Yes, they communicate essential information, but it's housed in a very frustrating, difficult-to-understand, oftentimes impossible-to-even-read-let-alone-digest form. It may never have even occurred to you that those types of documents don't have to be written that way.

The goal of all writing is to communicate—not to confuse and frustrate, and certainly not to put someone to sleep. Just because a legacy of failure has been in place for potentially hundreds of years doesn't mean that it needs to be extended and honored through your work.

Let me offer you a few examples of this.

the divine writer within

A number of years ago, a professor from the nursing department at the University of Tennessee contacted me. I had recently appeared at the university, but she had a scheduling conflict and as a result was unable to attend my lectures, so she asked if I would be able to work with her on an individual basis.

She and a colleague had written a book on the spiritual aspects of nursing, which they hoped to have published as a textbook and distributed nationally through colleges and universities. She paid me to review her manuscript and offer my assessment, which I did. At our consultation, I began our conversation by asking her how honest she wanted me to be about the quality of her book.

"Absolutely honest," she replied.

"Okay, then," I replied. "The bad news is that the book sucks because it's boring, but the good news is that I found about five sentences that work because they're passionate. All you have to do is rewrite the book from the same frame of mind you were in when you wrote those five sentences and then you'll have a great book."

"But it's a textbook," she responded.

"Just because all your other colleagues wrote boring books doesn't mean that you have to follow in their footsteps," I challenged.

To make a long story shorter: I worked with this professor for a considerable period of time to get her heart to come through in her writing. Once that was accomplished, she rewrote her book from that perspective and then submitted it to a collection of academic publishers who published her sort of text. Within a few weeks, three of them contacted her to offer contracts for her work, which was a great. However, what was even more affirming for me was the fact that those who offered her a contract conveyed basically the same information to her: They had been looking for a book like hers for quite some time, but each manuscript they received was written in a dull, dry, and boring textbook manner, which was exactly the opposite of what they felt would be appropriate for a work focusing on the spiritual aspects of nursing.

Pearl of *Wisdom*

Effective writing is the result of a direct interaction with the DWW. No matter what the topic, your writing doesn't have to be boring and unemotional. In fact, if it is, you have failed. You've failed to communicate because you failed to reach your reader through the sharing of yourself.

In another case, I worked with a tax attorney. Is there any more of an LCB-based profession than a tax attorney? Anyway, he wanted to write a novel and began to do so under my guidance, which all of sudden led him to change how he approached his writing at work. He was now in touch with his DWW (through the writing of his novel) and could transfer its magic over to his briefs at work. The result? He began to communicate more effectively and more humanly in the briefs he was writing to be presented in court.

By communicating more effectively, he was better able to substantiate his case to the judge he was appearing before. In fact, his message routinely outshined that of whatever opposition he ran up against and he began winning an unheard-of percentage of the cases he represented. As a result, he began to receive more appreciation in the workplace because his writing there began to better convey his message. No matter how LCB-based the content he had to work with may have been, he was conveying what he had to say in a much more heartfelt, passionate fashion. His writing became the cornerstone of the raises and promotions he would receive shortly afterward.

WRITING PRINCIPLE #14

Always Conclude a Writing Session in the Midst of a Section or Chapter

Why? Because if you conclude a writing session at the *end* of a chapter or section, you also bring to a conclusion the flow of your DWW through your CCB, at least for that portion of your writing. Starting from scratch to reconnect makes it ten times as difficult to begin

Sedona Secret
HOW TO BEGIN AND END A WRITING SESSION

The best-case scenario is that you connect with your DAW, write well, and conclude a writing session in the midst of a sentence, section, and/or chapter. Just before you begin the next session, reconnect with your DWW. Then rewrite the last twenty to thirty words you wrote during your previous session, which tunes you right back into the momentum and tone you had then.

writing the next day because you will have to create a DWW flow to attach onto.

So how do you ensure that it will be easy to pick up where you left off at the beginning of your next writing session? Stop mid-paragraph or even midsentence and somewhere in the midst of a section and chapter. That way, the flow will be openly exposed and much easier to connect with and pick up at the start of your next session. If you choose to use a specific time as your stopping point for your writing session, that's fine too. Just make sure that you don't stop at the conclusion of a chapter and/or section. Avoiding having to create a new flow every session will also limit the amount of "dead writing" in your work, which is sure to appear while you're warming up in an attempt to re-establish a DWW-based flow.

> **Don't conclude your writing sessions at the end of a chapter or section.**

WRITING PRINCIPLE #15

Reserve Time to Get to Know, Love, and Then Embrace Your Own Unique and Brilliant Creative Voice

How much time does that require? Three to five weeks—the amount of time it takes to write your first book using my method.

One important part of this principle—you can't read anything other than magazines, newspapers, and what you have to read for work or for a class you are taking. Other than that, no books. Yes, you heard me correctly. Don't read *any* books (other than the ones you have to read for work or for a class) during this short, but very important, period of your life.

I know, you're disagreeing with me and wondering why I've instituted this rule. Well, as a result of my many years of teaching, I knew many things about you before you picked up this book.

I knew that:

- You have wanted to write for a substantial period of time.
- You may have tried to shake this desire on many occasions, but weren't able to.
- Your momentum to pursue this task has grown every day.
- You may have even attempted to write a book or two on your own, or maybe you actually did complete some writing, but you weren't, for whatever reason, satisfied with the result.
- Your DWW has visited you on several occasions and everything seemed to work just right with your writing, but you weren't able to identify exactly what it was that happened, and as a result, you were unable to repeat it on a consistent basis.
- There is an extremely high probability that you like to read a lot, which, of course, is the result of you borrowing someone else's DWW connection to sublimate your own inability to connect.

The good news is that you don't need to try to emulate someone else's DWW once you can consistently connect with your own. In fact, you may have already begun feeling the difference. You may already know the difference I am referring to—the one that draws you less to the DWW connections of others through the reading of their books, and instead continually leads you off in the direction of your own connection to your writing. This change, of course, will save you hundreds of dollars annually in book purchases while potentially adding extra money to your pocket through publication.

Here are questions I get from students about this principle.

- *"Why discontinue reading right now and for such a long period of time?"* It's *not* a long period of time. In the entire spectrum of things, the time period I am referring to is a single drop of rain in a downpour.
- *"But why sever myself from something I love so much?"* There are two reasons for this. First, *because reading other writers' books*

would cause you to either emulate their styles or to be intimidated by them—neither of which is a good thing for your writing. Second, your LCB has not had enough uninterrupted time with your DWW to allow it to familiarize itself with your own creative voice so that it can finally accept it. So your LCB needs the chance to get to know your DWW and its brilliant and creative voice. Because your LCB automatically rejects that which it does not recognize, it has been rejecting your DWW and your unique, special voice. Give your LCB the chance it needs to get to know this wonderfully expressive DWW—reserve book-free time.

WRITING PRINCIPLE #16

Two Drafts Is All It Takes

You may have seen the movie *Finding Forrester* with Sean Connery. If you haven't seen it, watch it, because it's maybe the only movie on writing that at least moderately depicts, in a functional way, both the craft and those who participate in it. In the movie, Connery is a reclusive, famous author who changed people's lives with his first book and then disappears. Accidentally (even though there are no accidents in life), he is discovered by a young man in his Bronx neighborhood who wants to, of course, write. Eventually, they become each other's mentors. The young man teaches Connery about himself and life, while Connery counsels the young man on writing.

There is a scene in the movie that accurately depicts what I am referring to with Principle #16. The young man and Connery are facing each other across a desk. Connery commands the young man to begin writing, which he is unable to do. So Connery demonstrates for the young man what he means and he just begins doing so, all the while he is still carrying on a conversation with his pupil, saying something along the lines of the following:

"The first draft is all heart," he says, as he continues writing. "The second draft is where you use your head."

Exactly.

Write your first draft completely and totally from your DWW. In your second and final draft, you'll utilize your LCB's skills, under the watchful and patient eye of your strengthened CCB, of course. If you allow a direct, monogamous connection with your DWW in your first draft, there will be no need for extensive follow-up drafts. In truth, those are no more than attempts to find the heart in your writing that you had somehow left out in your first run-through. Remember:

And if they're all there, you simply have to revise your material along the lines I suggest in Chapter 6 and you will be done.

> **If the heart is in your first draft, so is the depth and direction necessary to form a book.**

Pearl of Wisdom

Another reason to avoid going beyond a second and final draft is that the more drafts beyond the second one that you write, the more frustrated, at least subconsciously, you will become with the book. This frustration will show in how you attack your writing (yes, from the second draft on you will be attacking it).

WRITING PRINCIPLE #17

You Don't Have to Be Highly Educated, or Even Proficient, in Spelling, Punctuation, and Grammar to Be a Successful Writer

If that weren't the case, every English teacher/professor and librarian would be a bestselling author. The key to all successful, communicative writing directly springs from your ability to tap into your heart (DWW) and then release it through your CCB. It's not from serial commas or proper capitalization.

If you're anything like me, you slept through session after session on grammar, punctuation, and spelling. Never before had I run into material so dry and boring and that appeared to be such a waste of my time. That's not to say that learning to spell, punctuate properly, and master grammar is a waste of anyone's time. Nothing could be further from the truth. However, since I was taught about it far before I needed it in my writing, I never saw a need for it.

And then because of my long, drawn-out exposure to it, when I was finally given the chance to do some writing in school, it appeared as if punctuation, spelling, and grammar were at the core of any good writing. After all, that's what my teachers focused on and based a large part of my grade on. Of course, I discovered that grammar and spelling are not even close to being at the core of good writing. Sure, they are important, but they are nothing unless the writing they are applied to has been released passionately and directly from one's heart. They will help refine that essence. They will help better communicate it, but they are not that essence.

So, if you're anything like me, and your grasp of the technical factors of writing is a bit remedial, so what? You can buff that up with a little bit more study in that area, a copyeditor, or grammar- and spellcheck. But nobody, absolutely no one, will ever be able to replace the special DWW gift you bring into this world through your CCB and DWW's unique, one-of-a-kind expressive voice.

Conclusion

Once you have effectively read and understood the seventeen principles and completed the accompanying exercises, you are ready to move on to the release of your book. Through it, you will be able to see just how much you have learned, how much you have grown, and how brilliant and wonderful you are.

chapter four

Commitment

CONTRARY TO WHAT you may have been told or may have thought about yourself, you don't lack commitment. Not only have you probably progressed from grade to grade, graduated from schools, held down jobs, paid off loans, perhaps even successfully loved and raised children, you have learned a lot about yourself through the completion of the exercises in the first three chapters. In addition, you have not given up on your dream to write, and, most importantly, you are reading this book in order to do something about it. Bravo!

Pearl of *Wisdom*

You are already very brave and very committed. From my perspective, you don't have to commit *more*. Moving forward, you simply need to commit more *wisely*, which means writing a contract with yourself.

The Contract

There is one common denominator among all the commitments you have followed through on in your life. That common denominator is an agreement that you have entered into, either formally or informally, with yourself and most probably with an outside source as well—I'm talking about mortgages, marriages, and so on.

As far as this contract is concerned, you can write it in longhand, type it out, whatever—it doesn't matter as long as it is committed to paper, copied, and distributed in the manner I'll explain shortly. All of this, including mailing it, will cost you less than $5 and take you less than a few hours, travel time included.

Why You Need a Contract

The need for this contract is very real. You may have been talking about writing a book for years and your LCB has heard every one of your claims, which up to this point have been nothing more than empty promises. As a result, your LCB doesn't believe you when you say you're going to write a book. Can you blame it? All that it has experienced up to this point are a bunch of empty promises. Remember, your LCB has led you to every success in your life and you need to get it on your side now so it can lead you to the success you seek as a writer.

But frankly, it has grown skeptical of your claims. It needs something firm and tangible, a document to verify that you are actually going to do something this time. That's where the contract comes in. Do it and you will, in all likelihood, succeed. Avoid it and, in all likelihood, you won't.

Tips for Writing a Successful Contract

Here are a few hints to help you create an effective contract:

- It should convey as much passion as possible.
- It should showcase a general statement of purpose, which basically answers the question, "What are you promising to do?"

USE A CONTRACT

Some form of contractual agreement is always the difference between success and failure. So wouldn't it make sense that if you wanted to succeed at writing a book that you should enter into a contract as well?

- Include a timeframe in which you will complete your book. For your purposes, writing six days a week and two hours a day at a writing speed of 1,500 words an hour, give yourself five weeks, which translates to thirty days of actual writing.
- Clearly state what you will receive on a daily basis if you complete your writing goals and what you will *not* get if you don't. This will do more than anything else to get your LCB on your side. Make sure that you are not being wimpy and weak here. Take away that glass of wine at the end of the day, or that bit of chocolate after dinner, or your cups of morning coffee if you don't complete your writing assignment. All you need to miss is one session and the LCB will quickly learn that when you write you get good things and when you don't, you experience pain of some sort. Thus, with its primary purpose being to lead you away from pain, your LCB will immediately reverse its approach to writing and begin leading you to it as opposed to leading you away from it.
- To cement your efforts to complete the writing of your book, make absolutely no provisions for failure by not meeting your goals on time.
- Your agreement needs to be signed and dated.
- Once your contract is complete, make seven copies of it. Keep the first copy for yourself and ensure that it's in view each and every time you write. Send the second copy to me at *TomBird@ TomBird.com*, which will comprise a formal rite of passage to your LCB. Then take the next three copies and send one to three people whom you consider tough-love specialists. You know, the ones who would remind you the rest of your days if you fell short of your goal. For God's sake, why send to them? Because their presence will do more to motivate your LCB to keep you on track than anything else. The last two copies? Send them to two people who love you unconditionally, who won't be anywhere near as motivating because they'll love you whether you succeed or not, and as a result your LCB won't be motivated nearly as much by them.

Sample Contracts

Here are some sample agreements to give you some ideas.

Individual Agreement #1

Writer's
REFLECTION

Make a list of the people in your life who will receive a copy of your contract and which category of person each is (tough love, unconditional love). Create a short speech or letter that will accompany this person's copy of your contract that explains what you're doing and what you need them to do.

On this seventh (7th) day of October in the year 2009, I (Author), do enter into this contract willingly and with full knowledge of what is expected of me by me. I write this contract in order to commit myself to writing a book, a book that is presently inside me now. I will complete this book by Thanksgiving of the year 2009. I do understand the necessity of this contract binding me to a commitment of writing.

I will reserve two hours daily, six days a week, to write.

I will remove all distractions. I will set boundaries for those near and dear to me and ask them to respect those boundaries so that I may have uninterrupted time.

I will do relaxing exercises before writing, while writing, and after writing.

I will allow my thoughts and feelings to flow freely onto blank, lineless paper.

On a daily basis, I will reward myself for having accomplished my writing goals.

When I have finished my final copy and have sent it off to a literary agent, I will travel to Sedona and spend the day, complete with a picnic lunch of my favorite foods, on the back side of Oak Creek Canyon. I will take pictures and rejoice in my favorite place.

I gladly and willingly and most excitedly do sign this contract.

_____

Author

_____

Date

Individual Agreement #2

On this day of November 24, 2009, I hereby openly make clear my intentions to finally complete the book that has been keeping me up for years, and to start on my heartfelt career as a self-supporting author.

My plan of action will be this:

1. I will rise every morning at least ninety minutes before I usually get up, follow the Three Rs of Writing to put me in the proper mood, and then follow the appropriate directions from *The Call of the Writer's Craft*. By doing this, I plan to have my first book by January 24, 2010.

2. By no later than January 25, 2010, I will begin individually contacting literary agents.

3. With this plan in mind, I will land the proper agent for my book by no later than February 27, 2010.

4. Any revenues raised from the sale of my first book, or any that follow, will be placed in a special bank account established for the sole purpose of accumulating enough money for me to resign from my position at the bank and go to work on my writing full time.

5. As far as my routine and writing are concerned, I will stick with the aforementioned routine six days a week, each morning—moving from book to book—until I have earned enough to resign from my position. At that time, I will then follow the same routine with the Three Rs of Writing and devote myself to painting a minimum of five hours a day, with time put aside each day for the sales of my work.

I realize the importance of each person to whom I have sent a copy of this contract, and I call upon each one to police my heartfelt efforts in whatever way he or she chooses. If at any time I fall short of any of the goals listed above, and their corresponding deadlines, I hereby promise to treat each person who received a copy of this contract to a dinner at his or her favorite restaurant.

John Smith

Exercise: Write Your Contract

Digest the information and examples you've just read, and write your own personalized contract. Be sure you schedule deadlines and rewards for successful writing sessions.

the divine writer
within

I was once approached by a woman on the way to a lecture. Since she caught me in the midst of a daydream-like state while she was in a very excited state, I was initially taken back by her sudden appearance. She told me how she had come to register for my class that evening. She had a friend who had taken one of my classes previously. Like all writers who want to make the leap but who aren't quite ready to do so yet, this woman watched as her buddy executed the suggestions I had made, including writing a contract. The friend had given one of the copies of her contract to the woman who was now speaking with me.

"And you know what happened?" she asked me.

"No," I replied.

"Well, she finished the book," she went on. "But the most amazing part of the story is that she finished her long-awaited book on exactly the day that she said she would in her contract. My friend wasn't aware of this fact, though, since she had stuffed her own copy of the contract in a desk drawer (yes, she was supposed to have it in plain view . . . but clearly just the act of writing it was enough for this particular woman, since she finally finished her book!). But I made her aware of it the minute she finished. At first, she didn't believe me. But then she fished through the drawer for the copy of the contract she had crammed in there. And, boy, was she surprised to see that

> "The actor becomes an emotional athlete."
>
> Award-winning actor and Sedona resident Al Pacino

the date she stated on the contract, by which time she would have the book done, was the exact day that she completed it. It was as if the book, itself, had written the contract to make her aware of where the two of them were going and when it would conclude writing itself through her."

Conclusion

You may feel unnecessarily formal writing a contract, but it's an essential part of the program. Remember, it doesn't make you commit *more*, it just makes you commit more *wisely*.

"Life is hard; but it's harder if you're stupid."

Actor and former Sedona resident John Wayne

"It's a helluva start, being able to recognize what makes you happy."

Former Sedona resident and
acclaimed actress Lucille Ball

chapter five

Guaranteeing
Your Success

LET'S GO OVER the checklist that will guarantee that you will
have everything you need for the grand and glorious journey that
writing your book will be.

What to Do Before You Begin

Here's a quick checklist that highlights some of the most important
things we've talked about over the last four chapters:

- ❑ Send out all your contracts, especially the one meant to go to me.
- ❑ Arrange a weekly writing schedule of no less than two hours a day,
  six days a week.
- ❑ Warn those in your life or with whom you share a home or office, or
  wherever you write, about the private time you need and tell them
  that you will enforce your rights in this regard.

Things to Keep in Mind While Writing

Here are the things to keep in the front of your mind at all times
about your writing experience. Read over the following list at least

once a week, and immediately if you run into a problem or a stoppage with your writing. If that happens, turn to this page right away and read over the list to see which of the suggestions you have innocently forgotten to implement. Put that procedure back into practice, and get back to your writing.

1. Always precede any writing, or reading of your writing, by first following the Three Rs of Writing.
2. Always write as fast as you can.
3. Remember to warm up at the beginning of each writing session by recopying the last twenty to thirty words that you wrote at your previous session.
4. Just let the words fly out of you, allowing your DWW to take you and your writing wherever you are both destined to go.
5. Do not edit, review, or read your work as you are writing.
6. Leave gaps for any bits of information or facts that you may need to research later.
7. If any potentially distracting thoughts pop into your mind, dump them into a narrow column on the right side of each of your pieces of paper.
8. No matter how much preparatory work you have done up to this point, you'll still not know where you are going with your writing from day to day. Remember, this is your DWW's way of keeping you interested.
9. Never conclude a writing session at the end of a chapter or section.

Sedona Secret
TAKE A NAP!

Whenever Thomas Edison used to run into a problem with one of his inventions, he used to take a catnap. You see, Edison believed that when one slept, his or her soul left the body and went to a higher level of consciousness, and then it came back and re-entered the body upon re-awakening, bringing back with it whatever information it was lacking or needed to know. You may find Edison's theory helpful with your writing.

A Few Last-Minute Insights

1. The writing of any major project usually starts off slowly. In fact, it is not unusual for your DWW to switch back and forth between the first or third person in the beginning. Until you both get used to each other, don't allow any early sluggishness to rattle you. Be assured that your connection will smooth out eventually.

2. You may find yourself starting to fall asleep during your writing sessions. This is not because your writing is boring. This is happening because your CCB is reaching up to your DWW for a higher level of understanding, which it can't quite reach while you are in a waking state. So if you feel as if you want to go to sleep during a writing session, allow yourself to do so. Just put your head down on your desk and nod off. In no time at all, you will wake back up with a renewed vigor and point of view that wasn't there before falling asleep. (Note: the time spent napping doesn't count as part of your two hours of writing time.)

Pearl of *Wisdom*

Remember that all you need to know, you already know, and all you need to have, you already have in your possession. To remind yourself of this fact, all you have to do is to look back through this book at all that you have already accomplished.

3. To help ease the concerns of your LCB, you may want to use the last five minutes of each writing session to jot down where your DWW, communicating through your CCB, sees you going the next day. That way, with a roadmap of at least the next day's destination squarely in front of it, your LCB won't feel so lost and out of control.

4. You may also want to reserve the last ten minutes or so before you stop to do some brainstorming on paper. Doing so espe-

cially helps to prime your DWW to really take off the next session. In fact, if you experience any sluggishness at the beginning of your writing sessions, you will find that doing this usually cures you of it.

5. Since the part of you that you'll connect to when writing affects you and those you are connected most closely with, it is not unusual to experience a short period of time, shortly after beginning on a book, when other parts of your life seems to be falling apart. If that happens to you, don't overreact. Everything and everyone will calm down in a few days as they adjust to the massive amount of new energy you're allowing to enter into your life, through your writing.

6. If you happen to fall off your writing schedule for a few days, don't plan to jump back in where you left off without a hitch. You may need to first address and release some personal issues first, through your writing, before you can do so.

7. Your project will end on its own. You will be given very little advance notice of when this will happen. Just a few minutes before it concludes is usually the norm. The reason for this short notice is so that your LCB will not have time to come out and screw up your execution.

General Points to Keep in Mind at All Times

When writing your first book:

1. Work on your writing two hours a day, six days a week, no matter what happens.
2. Consistently pat yourself on the back, with some sort of reward, after the completion of each successful writing session.
3. Outside of required reading for your job or for a class, and magazines and newspapers, don't do any reading while completing your book.

Writer's REFLECTION

It is now time to clear the way for your book to come rolling right out of you:

1. Get into your DWW/CM-connected state.
2. Pull out a piece of your chosen writing surface, and in the center of it, write the working title of your book.
3. Allow yourself to completely free-associate any thoughts or feelings, whether they are directly tied to what you will be writing or not, by releasing them onto the lineless piece of paper, and making sure to circle each expression and then connect each circled item to the nearest item to it with a straight line. Remember just to allow these expressions to fly out of you as fast as you can.
4. Sometime in between eight and fifteen minutes of doing this, you will feel a strong and consistent stream of consciousness coming through you. Go to another piece of lineless paper, and, while following the rules above, allow the stream of consciousness, which will be your book, to come streaming out of you. Stay with this stream of DWW consciousness for an average of two consecutive hours before reconnecting with it the next day, the day after that, and however many days it takes after that until your book, all on its own, comes to a conclusion.

---

the divine writer within

After following my method, Michael Cohen of Manhattan not only wrote his first book, working two hours a day, six days a week, in less than three weeks, but he went on to complete a total of seven books in less than a year. Not only did he transition from wanting to be an author to being one, but everything in his life changed for the better. A direct connection with your DWW will do that.

In fact, my experience has shown me that there is no one more unhappy than a writer who should be writing and more unhappy than one called to do so who isn't following through on his/her soul purpose.

Conclusion

What are you waiting for? Get writing!

chapter six

The Final Draft for This Phase of Your Life

AFTER WRITING FOR about two hours a day, six days a week, you will have completed the first draft of your book in thirty days or fewer. At that point, more than 85 percent of what you set out to do will be completed.

While you work on the final draft of your book, you will be spending your "writing" sessions with the following steps. Even though these activities are vastly different from the steps you have taken to get the first draft down on paper, it is still important that you make sure to follow the Three Rs of Writing before beginning any session. Also keep in mind that each of the following steps may take up to several days to complete. When you are done with these steps, you will be finished with your book.

An Essential Point During This Draft

Somewhere during this last draft, the idea for your next book will pop out. Do not ignore it! In fact, when it appears, begin reserving one-third of the time you have allotted to revise your manuscript to release your second book onto large, lineless pieces of paper. Begin doing so by using the circle drawing exercise I described on page 29. Then just let it flow.

> **Pearl of** *Wisdom*
>
> Reserving time to release your next book is essential because it counterbalances the stiffness of the LCB-based revising you're doing. Circle drawing about your next book will enable you to glide through the revisions with greater ease. So don't forget: when that next book shows up, devote a certain portion of your time each day to letting it out.

Step #1: Noting (and Then Making) Structural Changes

Begin your review and revision of your manuscript by entering into your DWW-connected state. While in touch with your DWW, you can keep your LCB's influences to a minimum throughout this process. Once you're connected, read through your book, noting all major changes you would like to make.

I define major changes as any alterations, rearrangements, subtractions, or additions that directly affect the general theme or direction of what you have already written. This does not include grammatical changes and/or the correction of typographical mistakes.

the divine writer within

Literally every aspiring author whom I have mentored with the Tom Bird Method says nearly the exact same thing on the eve of entering into this phase: "There is no way that what I wrote can be any good. I wrote it too fast. So I am sure that it really stinks. To be honest, I don't really know what I wrote anyway—because, again, I wrote it too fast."

Each and every one was hesitant about moving forward with this step—yet, each and every one came away singing a completely different tune after taking a glimpse of his or her finished rough draft.

Take it from this student, who experienced a complete turnaround, a 180-degree shift: "Wow, I can't believe how good it is. In fact, I can't believe I actually wrote it. It's great, and it just seems to flow. I can't wait to get back to reading it. I am just so pumped to finish it." The reason for their turnarounds? Every time you make a shift within your writing by moving from one type of activity (say, writing) to another (say, revising), you lose your DWW's flow, which had been carrying you. Thus, the door opens for your LCB to creep back in and once again take control of your consciousness. Your LCB's reappearance is the soul (oops, sole) reason that you go from loving your book as you are writing it to despising it once you think about reviewing it.

Doubt (and Your LCB) Creep In

Because this process is LCB-focused, you're likely to encounter some of its influences along the way. Don't worry, though: All you need to do to move beyond your LCB's reaction is to calm it down, put it back to sleep (using the Three Rs of Writing), and then start reading. As you reconnect with the flow of your DWW, your review of your book will become as exciting and fun as the writing of it.

The Post-It Method

The easiest way I have found to note structural types is to write down suggestions on Post-it notes, and then stick the notes on your large, lineless pages, wherever you're suggesting a change be made. Try using four different colors of small Post-it notes:

1. One color for the alterations you want to make in the text (e.g., changing a character's name or the way one character meets another)
2. A second color for any rearrangements you want to make (e.g., moving chunks of text around)
3. The third color for additions to the text
4. The fourth color for subtractions/cuts

Marking all the changes you want to make will likely take approximately four days' worth of writing sessions. After you've gone through your manuscript and color-coded each change you want to make, you can begin making the changes. Just go through page by page, picking off one Post-it after another. Actually making your edits could take a week or more of writing sessions.

Step #2: Postwriting Research

Fill in all the research gaps you left in your manuscript. As I mentioned in Principle #12, it's better to write your book, then go back and research only those facts and figures that you actually need. Now is the time to do that. The time you need for this step will vary widely, depending on the type of book you're writing—a romance novel will likely need less research than a compilation of interviews. After you have completed this task—in most cases, it'll take you about a week—move on to the next step.

> "It's a total surprise. I don't have any concerns about the product."
>
> Dancer and Sedona resident Ann Miller

Step #3: Review Your Sentence Structure

No one will ever know the purpose and meaning of your work better than you and your DWW. This step is designed to not only fine-tune your manuscript but also to acclimate your LCB to the deepest,

Sedona Secret
DON'T RUSH

You may have to use several more pieces of large, lineless paper to work through your revisions. In addition, it may take several days to complete this task. Don't rush through this stage—you're doing important work to polish what you've written. Finish this step fully before moving on to the next step.

expressive abilities of your DWW. While your LCB and DWW are at odds most of the time, they *can* actually work in harmony too. Step #3 is one of those times. Your LCB is getting what it wants (it's following grammatical rules) and your DWW is still able to think creatively (to find better expressive word choices).

With that in mind, you need to be in charge of fine-tuning your manuscript. To do so, you will need a pack of four different colored highlighters. You'll use these highlighters to make six separate sweeps through your manuscript. Each sweep may comprise more than one writing session.

The First Three Passes

Here are the first three sweeps you'll need to make through your entire manuscript:

1. **Pass-through #1:** Highlight your action verbs with one highlighter.
2. **Pass-through #2:** Highlight all your passive verbs with a different color.
3. **Pass-through #3:** Use the last two markers to highlight all your adjectives and adverbs.

These three sweeps through your manuscript may take days. If you are confused and unsure on these different forms of language, go back and brush up on your grammar. I know, in Principle #17, I said you don't have to be an expert, but you do need a fundamental knowledge of good writing in order to polish your book.

The Last Three Passes

Once you have completed those three highlighting sweeps, go through your manuscript a fourth time, and focus solely on finding your action verbs. Ask yourself if each and every action verb is the most appropriate and expressive one possible. If it's not, change it as necessary. For example, did you use "said" too much? Are there places you could instead use "yelled," "whispered," "sighed," or "cried"? While you don't want to overdo it with expressive verbs, they are very powerful if used appropriately.

After you have completed your work with the action verbs, make the fifth sweep and focus solely on your passive verbs. The problem with passive verb construction is that it carries absolutely no imagery and is vague. Thus, they rob the reader of his or her ability to feel, hear, see, smell, or taste in reaction to your work. Too many passive verbs, especially one after another, will bore your reader. Of course, you don't want to do that. So, ask yourself, in each case, if there is a way you could possibly alter your sentences and/or paragraphs to rid your manuscript of so many passive verbs, and substitute action verbs in their place. For example, instead of saying "Dinner was made by Tom," consider something like, "Tom sautéed herbed chicken and summer squash."

On your sixth and final sweep, pluck out any adjectives and adverbs that you no longer need. In fact, they may be making your text redundant and, if left untouched, may lead to your project being "wordy."

Step #4: Type It In

Now it's time to type—or read, if you choose to use a voice activation program—your manuscript into your computer. For this, you will need an easel or some sort of structure that will secure your large pieces of paper at eye level.

Sedona Secret
REVIEW YOUR VERBS

Verbs are the pulse of each one of your sentences. They direct, project forward, and are responsible for creating the most imagery, which is what makes the reader *feel* something. When they are perfectly attuned, not only will your words sing, but a substantial portion of your adjectives and adverbs will have become obsolete as well. The verbs will carry the imagery without those extra words.

You're actually doing more than typing at this point, however. You're also keeping an eye out for any awkwardness that resulted from your work in Step #1. It's essential that you relax during this step. By being as relaxed as possible, your heightened sensitivity will enable you to sense and smooth out any disjointed aspects of your text that were caused by rearranging, add-

> "Going up the walls and doing somersaults, that trick took a couple of days."
>
> Donald O'Connor, costar with Gene Kelly in *Singin' in the Rain* and former Sedona resident

ing, subtracting, or making general adjustments to your material. When you have finished entering your manuscript into your computer, go on to the next step.

Step #5: Do One Final Read-Through

Once your manuscript has been typed into your computer, print out a hardcopy. As you read over your manuscript one last time, check for any last-minute adjustments that may need to be made. At this point, they will likely be small items, such as bits of text that need to be bridged, or in some cases, even relocated one last time. Finish reading through your manuscript one final time and then move on to the final section.

Pearl of *Wisdom*

During this final phase, you may find yourself feeling ambivalent. One part of you will be wildly excited to get this project completed, while the other side of you will be sad. This is normal. What you have written is like your literary child. There is a part of you that is anxious for your child to leave the nest, while there is another portion that is terribly sad at having to say goodbye. Keep in mind that your literary child will be with you always. No matter where the two of you venture from this point forward, the connection, love, and interchange that you've shared will always be a part of you.

Is My Book *Really* Done?

Even after all the revision work you've just completed, your book may need further polishing, sometimes by a professional editor. How do you know if that's the case? Here's what I suggest:

1. Find a reputable and suitable copyeditor. (Check out a source such as PublishersMarketplace.com to find one to ensure that who you are considering is a professional.)
2. Ask the person to edit a few pages of your book. Most copyeditors will do a sample edit of a few pages of your material to share with you exactly what they would be doing to your manuscript and how much work, if any, needs to be done.
3. Gauge the state of your book from their response to your work. If the person had many suggestions just on those few pages, the manuscript probably needs further editing. At that point, you want to consider either hiring the copyeditor, or finding a style editor, who would handle more big-picture editing (see pages 111–113 for more on style editors and copyeditors).

Conclusion

You have written a book. You are an author. I told you it was simple, didn't I? You wrote it in less than thirty days, did some revisions, and typed it into an electronic file. Now let's talk briefly about your next book before I show you how to sell this one!

Writer's
REFLECTION

Grab a piece of lineless paper, and write down everything you are feeling at this moment. Your book is complete—what a tremendous accomplishment! What would you like friends and family to say to you at this moment? What are you most proud of? What did you have to overcome? Who do you have to thank? Write until you have nothing else to share or celebrate. Embrace the good with the so-called bad. Was there anything that you had to leave behind to embrace your present circumstance? If so, write it down. You are stepping into the life you always wanted or have been called to live for so long. Congratulations!

chapter seven

Sharing Your First Book and Writing Your Second One

IN MY EXPERIENCE and that of my students', book number two will probably be streaming out of you at this point in the process. If you want to write that book now, then do so. If you would rather sell your first book first, your second will be waiting around for you whenever you want to plug back into it. By now, you certainly know how to do that.

If You Choose to Write Your Second Book

If you choose to write your second book using this system now, I have plenty of good news for you:

- Because of *"the dues"* you paid in getting beyond and above what was holding you back (all those Archetype appearances and so on), much of what you did previously to prepare for this journey doesn't need to be done again now. In fact, you can skip everything that preceded you actually writing your book. Yes, that's correct. There's no need to focus any further on the 17 Principles of Writing or redo those exercises.

- You can also skip doing a contract.
- You can read as many books as you want. Why? The time you set aside when you *didn't* read during the writing of your first work will have offered your LCB all the time it needed to get to know, and no longer reject, your own, unique DWW voice. You will no longer be trying to emulate someone else's style when you read other books. You've discovered and accepted your own voice.

Just keep writing the book, and go straight to the revision stage when you're done. Once there, do your read-through, make any necessary structural changes, finish your postwriting research, and then type your manuscript into your computer and perform your final read-through.

No, I didn't miss a step. *You won't have to do any of the enhancing with the markers and different parts of speech.* If you properly completed that phase with your first book, your LCB should have already been retrained to let your DWW choose the best words the first time around. You'll write your second book in a fine-tuned, deeply expressive, flowing writing style that best depicts your voice.

Sharing Your First Book

When you finish a book but have not yet officially published it, the worst thing you can do is to share it with anyone not qualified to read it. That's why I suggest that you restrict the prepublication sharing of you work to professional editors and literary

Writer's REFLECTION

Pull out your large, lineless drawing pad of paper. In the center of the paper write: *I am ready to write my next book NOW,* and circle it. Then write down the thoughts or feelings that come into your consciousness, circling each one immediately. Do not discriminate. Just let your feelings out. Within eight to twelve minutes, you will move through the staccato portion of the exercise and begin writing either/both long phrases and/ or sentences. Once you have moved to another lineless piece of paper you will be writing your next book.

agents only. (We'll cover how to find professional editors and literary agents in great detail in Part Two.) Doing so will keep you from exposing your recently born writing to someone who has never successfully held a literary baby in his arms or someone who is consciously (or subconsciously) jealous of that fact that you have one and he doesn't.

Sharing your book or writing with the world, including your family members, friends, and colleagues *after* it has been published, is another thing all together. Encourage them all to read it—that's what publication is for. Let people know you have written a book. If your mere mentioning of that fact spikes their interest, offer them some further information or give them a copy to read.

> "We cannot forever hide the truth about ourselves from ourselves."
>
> Senator and former candidate for president of the United States John McCain, who owns a home just outside of Sedona

Measuring Your Success

I do not feel that the success of an author is determined by whether he or she has been published and/or by how many books were sold as a result. I feel that the benefits of a book run much deeper and are way more valuable than that. However, at the same time, I feel as if you have a responsibility to share with others who could most benefit what the DWW released through you. As you can see, from the following, sharing what she wrote made all the difference for my student, Debbie Blais.

Sedona Secret
WRITING YOUR SECOND BOOK AND BEYOND

If you choose to continue to write books, you know what to do. Just follow what you did with the release of your second book and keep going, book after book after book.

the divine writer within

From: Deborah Tyler Blais, Florida, author of *Letting Your Heart Sing*
To: Tom Bird

My schedule is a little fuller than I anticipated, but I love it. After the book had been out about four months, the tide turned, and I no longer had to bang on doors, send e-mails, or make phone calls to book dates for book signings or talks. Word of mouth traveled fast, and people and organizations began vying for my time! Yesterday, I met Rosie O'Donnell and gave her a book (who knows where that may lead). And a member of one of my spiritual groups was a producer with the *Oprah* show for seven years. He LOVES the book and is doing everything he can to help me get the book on *Oprah*.

I can hardly keep up with the correspondence from readers and keep getting asked, "When is the workbook coming out?" I am currently working on it and expect it will be out next year. I don't know how this happened, but *Letting Your Heart Sing* made its way into a women's prison, and they have started a Bliss Group there and are using the tools in my book to change their lives, so that when they get out, they do not have to return to a life of crime. Instead, they can live the lives they were always meant to. I can't tell you how much joy and gratitude that brings me. So, Tom, in ways you can't even imagine, the work we did together continues to transform lives everywhere.

Sedona Secret
MUM'S THE WORD

If someone asks you to read her book before it's published, never offer insight or advice unless asked. The student should always seek the teacher, never vice versa. Unless the writer specifically asks you for editorial critique, simply congratulate the person on her accomplishment in finishing the manuscript.

I refer people to your web site constantly, so don't think I'm not thinking about you, I am. And I can't thank you enough for helping me fulfill my deepest heart's desire: to share my stories in such a way as to inspire others to follow their heart's desires, so that they too can experience the indescribable joy that comes from letting their heart sing.

Wow. Debbie's experiences postpublication have been life-altering! Your vision of success may be different from hers, which is fine. You can define and measure your own success however you like.

Conclusion

While you're likely proud to have a completed book ready to share, you likely can't do that on any large scale until you've published it. So let's move on to learning all the ins and outs of publication.

"Love yourself first and everything falls into line."

Former Sedona resident and acclaimed actress Lucille Ball

"It's busier and busier every day, but I really don't notice it. I get up every day and do what I love, so I can't complain. It's my dream job."

Award-winning vocalist and Sedona native Michelle Branch

part two

Getting Published

"If you can dream it, you can do it."

Frequent visitor to Sedona, Walt Disney

"A film is never really good unless the camera is in an eye in the head of a poet."

Former Sedona resident and acclaimed filmmaker and actor Orson Wells

chapter eight

What You Most Need to Know about Publishing

ENTIRE TOMES HAVE been written about how to get a book published. I'll boil down the essential information so you can quickly get your work represented and published in a manner that suits you and your work.

Before You Begin the Process: Remember Your Passion

Before I delve into the logistics of publishing your book, let me first speak to the most important facet of the whole process. What readers most want and what you most need to express is the passion of your own heartfelt purpose and/or message. That passion is what draws readers to read what they read, which in turn sells books, conveys a message, and changes the world.

Because you followed my method, you wrote from your heart. And writing from your heart means you wrote with the passion that will ensure that you succeed. If you had offered anything less, you would not only be failing your audience, but also yourself and your DWW connection.

the divine writer
within

I once worked with a student from South Florida in individual sessions. She realized the power of her passion, and it changed not only how she approached writing but her entire life as well.

She came to this understanding through hearing a bestselling author speak at a local bookstore. Before the book signing, the author made a small presentation to his audience and answered some questions. In the course of his presentation, someone asked how he had finally achieved his success after struggling as a writer for so long.

"I finally stopped listening to, and trying to adjust to, what everyone else wanted to me to write, and wrote only what I, myself, wanted to write. And that made all the difference," he said. "When I made the decision to write whatever I wanted to write, whether it got published or not, everything took off for me."

You see, up until that time, this well-known author had put aside his passion for what he thought other people wanted. He had no idea that what the readers really wanted was to experience the passion he was trying to subdue.

Pearl of *Wisdom*

Unfortunately, a lot of bad advice circulates regularly on writing, mostly by those who have been unsuccessful at the craft and/or those who just don't understand it. The worst advice of all is that a writer should write on whatever topic the market is buying (for example, "Write about vampires! Vampires are so 'in' right now!"). Nothing could be further from the truth. Always write what you're passionate about.

Don't Be Intimidated

Nothing in our culture is more influential than the written, and especially *published*, word. The published word is the foundation of everything you have been taught. As a result, no art form—not acting, sculpting, music, or painting—garners more respect than writing.

Because of all the esteem lauded upon it, people often lose perspective on what publishing really is. People equate it to personal and professional advancement; the expression of talent, passion, intelligence, and respect; and to a certain immortality, since a published work is destined to live forever. However, by its literal, simple definition, publishing is the preparing and issuing of material for distribution and/or sale to the public.

Sorry to burst yet another bubble. But that's all it is.

Through the ages, an aura of impossibility has been draped around publishing as the result of those who teach it having been so unsuccessful at approaching it themselves. Writers are taught to think it's a privilege only available to a select, chosen few. As a result, erroneously, most who consider publishing find themselves so intimidated by it by the time they finally consider it that they fail before they even begin. Instead of taking a good, hard, realistic look at the industry and their publishing options, they become too afraid to proceed. This is the most catastrophic mistake new writers can make.

The following sections cover the ins and outs of the three main options for

> "If you want a happy ending, that depends, of course, on where you stop your story."
>
> Former Sedona resident and acclaimed filmmaker and actor Orson Wells

publishing books (two of which I recommend). The more you learn about the industry, the less likely you'll be to fall prey to the mistakes and pitfalls experienced by most aspiring authors. (I'll get into the publication of articles, short stories and poetry in Chapter 9.)

Traditional Presses

Yes, I'm talking about the New York houses you've no doubt heard of. Or any of the thousands of other traditional publishers out there, from the very large to the very small. These are the companies you probably think of first when you consider publishing. And yes, these publishers no doubt perform this task—and have done it successfully for a long time. However, you still need to be sure they are a good match for you before considering them. Just because you recognize a publisher's name doesn't mean that they recognize what's best for you, your book, and your career as an author.

What a Conventional Book Publisher Does and Does Not Do

Let's first define what most houses will do for you and your book. Every house is different, but the following actions are pretty standard.

PUBLISH YOUR BOOK

These companies will fulfill the true definition of publishing: they will print your book and make it available to the public.

MANAGE YOUR CASH FLOW

A publisher will collect all monies for sales of your books. They will manage the accounting duties for your sales, paying all bills associated with your book, and then passing off your share of the profits to you (perhaps through your literary agent, which we'll talk about later).

EDIT YOUR BOOK

Stories abound about how legendary authors stumbled upon the right editor, and that one editor ended up being the driving force behind the success in that writer's career. But if you're relying on an

Sedona Secret
LEARN ABOUT DISTRIBUTION

When considering publishers, try to find out how they approach sales and distribution. You want to be sure that the person responsible for getting your book onto store shelves will share and convey the passion *you* feel for your book.

editor to make your book a success, you're placing responsibility for your own future in someone else's hands . . . and I already told you (in Writing Principle #2), that's a no-no.

Here's the situation in the industry today. In order to try to make more money, many publishers publish more titles per year than they used to. And if they publish more books, editors have more work to do. However, most houses, in an attempt to keep overhead low, have not increased the sizes of their editorial staffs to compensate for the increase in the number of books published. As a result, editors don't have the time they once had to transform you into a star.

Though she's not going to wave a magic wand, your editor will probably offer some suggestions on how to improve your manuscript. When editors make these suggestions, they're relying on their knowledge of the market for your book and their own creativity to supplement yours. Your book will likely undergo a "developmental" or "line" edit to address big-picture issues, and then a more detailed copyedit to check for typos. It's important to remember that the editor is on your side—you both want to create a great book full of passion that will sell.

SELL AND DISTRIBUTE YOUR BOOK

Traditional houses are responsible for the sales and distribution of your book, which is the process of getting it onto shelves at bookstores across the world (or onto webpages). Before a book lands on the shelf at a chain bookstore, for example, a salesperson had to convince that store's "buyer" to purchase copies of the book to sell to consumers. How they complete this task, though, depends on the publisher. Some publishers outsource distribution to a nationally known company who specializes in books, while others employ their own sales force. Some publishers use both methods to cover as many bases as they can.

MARKET AND PUBLICIZE YOUR BOOK

Before we move into this topic, let me make it clear: *Marketing, alone, does not make a book a bestseller.* There is no doubt that it helps,

> "Publicity can be terrible. But only if you don't have any."
>
> Actress and Sedona resident Jane Russell

but it cannot alone get your book on a bestseller list. In fact, many a publisher has spent hundreds of thousands of dollars on a chosen book only to see the work land in the bargain bin.

Marketing (usually paid advertising of some kind) and publicity (usually free media coverage, such as radio and TV show appearances) simply bring the release of a book to the attention of a certain influential audience. From that time forward, the book must stand on its own.

Believe it or not, the vast majority of conventional/traditional publishers rely on an author to do his or her own marketing. Gone are the days of huge marketing budgets, nationwide tours, and bookstore signings galore. Don't fool yourself into believing that if you sign on with a traditional publisher, your house will take care of your book's every promotional need.

Pearl of *Wisdom*

It is word-of-mouth "advertising" that is truly responsible for turning a book into a bestseller.

The same understaffing situation that plagues the editorial staff at a traditional publisher is also true of the marketing and publicity staff. Even if a traditional publisher does decide to get involved with the promotion of your book, there is an excellent chance that their tiny marketing and publicity staff can't effectively handle their workload. The publicist assigned to promote your book may be working on dozens of books at that same time, which of course limits the amount of work he or she can do for each title. In fact, the marketing/publicity staff at traditional publishers is oftentimes so inadequate that they outsource those duties to specialized firms.

That said, marketing and publicity departments at traditional publishers offer a number of benefits. They often have connections and contacts at large, well-known media outlets. Without those contacts, it may be nearly impossible to get a foot in the door at some famous magazines and TV shows. If the departments *are* able offer some support for a book, they'll write a press release and pitch your title to media outlets to try to get coverage for it. And even if they're not able to launch a full-scale campaign for a title, they'll often brainstorm with authors to point their own marketing/publicity efforts in the right direction.

DESIGN THE ARTWORK FOR YOUR BOOK

Traditional publishers absorb the responsibility of creating the artwork associated with your book—for both the interior and the cover/book jacket. There are pros and cons to this option. Your book will be designed by a professional who is trained in this area, but you may not have as much artistic control over how your product looks as you would like.

COMPLETE LEGAL FILINGS

Traditional publishers will copyright your book (usually in your name, depending on your contract) with the U.S. Library of Congress and take the responsibility for performing other small legal tasks, including procuring the ISBN for your book, which is like a social security number.

> "Scarface—first you get the money, then the power and then you get the women."
>
> Award-winning actor and Sedona resident Al Pacino

However, they will not take responsibility for offering you any sort of legal protection if you're sued by a reader. In fact, as part of your contract, they may ask you to sign a waiver granting them immunity from any problems you run into. Contrary to misguided popular beliefs, traditional publishers do not protect you against being sued for what is offered in your book.

SELL "RIGHTS"

Part of a traditional publisher's role is to serve as a clearinghouse for the rights to your book. For example, a traditional publisher may purchase the hardcover rights for your book. But it may also serve as the agent to sell other "rights" to the book to other publishers, such as:

- Paperback rights
- Serial rights (the reprinting of excerpts from your book in magazines and newspapers)
- Book club rights

For their role in any transaction of this sort, they normally expect to receive a hefty percentage of all revenues generated (up to 50 percent). Thus, if your publisher sells the paperback rights to your book to an outside house, they will receive a 50 percent commission on all monies earned through their sale. So, if you agree to accept an 8 percent royalty rate for your paperback version, you will receive a whopping $.32 per book sold.

LEND CREDIBILITY

Because of their long-standing reputations and place in the publishing industry, traditional publishers, more than anything else, lend credibility to the name of, especially, the new author.

Other Aspects of Working with Traditional Publishers

Besides the who-does-what of an arrangement with a publisher, you'll need to understand a few other parts of the business as well.

YOU'LL LIKELY NEED A LITERARY AGENT

Even though it is not an absolute must in every case, the vast majority of all traditional publishers (including all the top publishing houses) refuse to review any material written by a new writer who is not represented by a literary agent. This rule is in place so publishers can rely on agents as a first "screening" and only review material that's passed their muster. We'll talk more about agents in Chapters 9 and 10. An agent's total take is normally 15 percent of your gross revenue, plus reimbursement of all his or her out-of-pocket expenses.

ADVANCES AND ROYALTIES

If a traditional publisher wants to publish your work, you will be offered an advance. I define an advance as "risk money applied against potential royalties earned." It's called an "advance" because the publisher sees it as "fronting" you money while you write the book. It will, however, deduct that money from your future earnings.

Here's how it works. Royalty rates can be based either on the book's cover price or on the *net* return received by the publisher (the net amount would include a large discount off the cover price given to bookstores who agree to sell your book). But, in that case, you would normally receive a much higher royalty rate to compensate for the discount afforded a bookstore or distributor. That's why royalty rates range between 5 percent and 25 percent.

Let's say that you accept a $10,000 advance from a publisher, your book eventually sells for $20, and you agree to a 10 percent royalty rate (which is based on the $20 cover price of the book). For each book sold, you would receive $2. So how many books would you need to sell to make back the advance you were offered? Correct: 5,000.

What would happen if your book sold only 3,000 copies? Would you then be responsible for returning $4,000? Legally, you are liable for the return of the unearned portion of the advance. However, if you have fulfilled your obligations as outlined under your contract with the publisher (submitting your manuscript on time, for example), rarely would you be expected to repay any part of your advance.

EARNINGS

Let's use the previous scenario to sketch out how much money you would actually receive from the sale of your book. Let's say your book sells the lofty total of 60,000 copies (which would be very impressive!). You would receive $120,000, minus your agent's commission of 15 percent, for a total of $102,000. (This total, of course, does not include the monies generated by your publisher for outside sales to book clubs, paperback rights, and so on.)

How much is pocketed by your publisher? If you sold 60,000 of your books on a straight 40 percent discount rate to stores (which is the standard discount at major bookstore chains), their gross revenue per book would end up being $12. However, you must deduct their production costs (for buying paper, printing, and shipping the books) of say, $3, and $2 for your advance, so they would end up clearing $7 per book (the publisher would have to subtract their in-house overhead from that figure to determine their final profit, but that's what they'd clear prior to that). That's two or three times as much money as you were awarded for actually writing the book.

Remember: It's a Business

In today's world, the vast majority of publishing houses are owned by corporations. Unfortunately, most of those corporations care about nothing other than the bottom line. If you think of it that way, traditional publishers are like venture capitalists. They are willing to absorb a high risk on each of their dollars invested in exchange for a potential high return.

Publishers are in the business to make money—period. They are not interested in influencing society or nurturing the career of a bright new writer, unless doing so would offer them a high return on their investment dollar. How much bottom-line revenue you and your book are worth, then, is their main consideration. One of the ways that you can become more attractive to them is directly tied to what you will do to market your own book.

So important is your willingness to directly contribute in this area that some publishers may expect you to state up front, before your book is considered for publication, how much you will be willing to offer marketing-wise toward the promotion of your own work. By limiting the monies they are expected to kick in to get more book sales, they also limit their liability. As a result, the $2 per book you could earn looks even smaller. This is especially the case if you decide to hire a professional publicity/marketing firm to promote your book. The rates for any of these firms usually range from $32,000 to $45,000.

For example, if you grossed the $102,000 via your 60,000-book sale stated earlier, and had to spend $40,000 promotionally, you would then have earned only $62,000, while your traditional publisher would have taken in $420,000: exactly the type of return a venture capitalist would expect.

Self-Publishing via Vanity Press

Self-publishing is not the dregs to which the failed writer is left to retreat. Quite the contrary, self-publishing is a great option for a great many writers. Just ask literary legends Mark Twain, James Joyce, D. H. Lawrence, Stephen Crane, Edgar Allan Poe, Rudyard Kipling, Walt Whitman, George Bernard Shaw, Ezra Pound, Henry David Thoreau, Zane Gray, Carl Sandburg, and John Grisham—all of whom self-published at one time. Although self-publishing via vanity press has been a popular alternative for certain trendsetters, it's an option littered with drawbacks.

It's Expensive

Until recently, the cost to produce a book was normally outside what an average American would want to spend. When self-publishing first began, it might cost tens of thousands of dollars just to have a manuscript typeset. Add to that the cost of a qualified content editor and you were easily in the $30,000 range. Also, in the past, to bring down the cost-per-unit price of one's book, authors had to agree to high-quantity first print runs of 10,000 copies or more. So, the author would have no choice but to sink at least another $40,000 into inventory, bringing his initial cash outlay to around $70,000. Ouch!

Nowadays, the costs at vanity presses *are* lower—up to several thousand, due up front. That fee usually does not include any promotion—no book- or author-specific website and no marketing campaign (though, for another fee, some will also print some promotional materials for you).

Authors Lack Control

A vanity press will design the book's layout and cover, buy an ISBN number, and fulfill orders. The book is published under the vanity press's name, and in some cases, the author must sign a contract ensuring that sell he will the book only through the press. All of this means that the author has very little control over each stage and may not know exactly how many copies have been printed or sold.

Books Get Poor Distribution

Even if an author does manage to front that money and self-publish and somehow end up with a saleable product, getting it in bookstores and distributed across the country is a whole new problem. In most cases, the future of a worthy book dies on the dusty shelves in the author's garage or attic.

Many Vanity Presses Are Crooked Companies

As the result of, and because of, an author's general lack of understanding and desperation, these seemingly attractive "vanity" or "subsidy" presses prey on authors. They claim that they can do all that needs to be done better and at a much lower price than doing it on one's own. However, these presses, long the poisons of academics and vulnerable senior citizens, receive the poor reputation they have for a reason.

Yes, they produce books—but these works are often poorly edited, poorly designed, and rarely ever promoted. As well, normally only enough copies were printed to soothe the author's fledgling ego. The shoddy work ensured that the vanity or subsidy houses could keep as much of the initial fee charged to the author as possible. Sure, authors are often allowed as much as a 75 percent royalty rate, which is amazingly attractive compared to traditional publishing houses. However, no matter how you look at it, 75 percent of 0 books sold is still $0.

> "Most of you probably never heard of me."
>
> Actress and Sedona resident
> Debbie Reynolds

The extraordinary royalty rate is like the scent of blood to a hungry shark. Once the hopeful author is reeled in, the vanity or subsidy publisher simply focuses on getting the job done quickly and cheaply so as to keep as much of the fee charged to the writer as possible. The potential profit from promotion was too slight to be considered even remotely attractive—especially when the next hungry sucker with the wide-open checkbook might be waiting eagerly around the bend.

Today's Self-Publishing: Print on Demand

Though it may only have been by the sheer quality of their works and the divine guidance associated with them, the authors mentioned on page 105 actually made it. The divine guidance for some, in today's market, is now referred to as Print On Demand presses, or POD publishing.

With the advent of widespread computer use, much has changed in the publishing industry. The cost of typesetting a book, now commonly referred to as formatting, has dropped from tens of thousands of dollars to around the $1,500 range. The computer age has also enabled books to be stored in the memory of a computer and to be summoned at any time—the best time being when someone is ready and willing to purchase it, "on demand." Thus evolved the name for this type of publishing alternative. Because of the computer age, a book can literally be called forward from memory and generated at the request of a buyer or potential purchaser. As a result, the author does not have to purchase a huge amount of inventory either, eliminating costly expense number two. The cost to self-publish a book dropped from $70,000 to around $2,000 to $3,000.

Most POD presses also offer you a turnaround time (from receiving your manuscript and transforming it into a fully published book) of less than thirty days. (Traditional presses take on average of between nine to thirteen months to perform the same task.)

Add to that the fact that the most influential wholesale distributor of books in the world, Ingram, through its offshoot Lightning Source, has spearheaded this jolt to the industry by opening its own POD press (see *www.lightningsource.com* for more information).

What a POD Publisher Does and Does Not Do

As a result of accepting the reins of being your own publisher, the POD press becomes your printing house with distribution capabilities. This, of course, is what self-publishing houses (including vanity or subsidy presses) have always been. However, in the past, these cagey creatures have been able to pass themselves off as more and thus, charged more than they were worth. The POD route is fast, efficient, and inexpensive, and is probably the most honest and forthright business deal yet offered the literary author/entrepreneur.

PUBLISH YOUR BOOK

POD presses will print your book and make it available to the public.

MANAGE YOUR CASH FLOW

Many POD companies, though not all, will provide accounting support for your book.

EDITING

This is up to you—PODs will not edit your book. You can, however, hire outside editorial help if you feel your book needs it.

SALES AND DISTRIBUTION

The best POD presses are directly tied into distribution companies, such as Ingram. However, sales and distribution of self-published books can be a big challenge. The fact remains that many major chains simply do not carry many self-published books. However, they will carry any self-published book if there is a demand for it (remember, they are in the business of selling books), which is where your awareness of book promotion comes into play. A good way to get people talking about your self-published book is to sell them directly to attendees at talks, workshops, or seminars you may give. If those who purchase your book like it, they will begin to talk about it with others, and in no time you may discover that bookstores begin ordering and stocking it as a result of the demand. These so-called "back-of-the-room" sales may prove to be both a very profitable and promotional option for your book. However, the reality exists that even though there are certainly some standout self-published bestsellers, the vast majority do not sell well enough (oftentimes because the author does not do his/her job promotionally) to entice a bookstore to take a chance on it.

MARKETING
This chore is your responsibility as well.

DESIGNING THE ARTWORK
This is up to you to get done if you work with a self-publisher. You will have to supply the POD press with your artwork in the exact electronic form that they require. Depending on your technical acumen, this task could be challenging and you'll likely need outside help (which we'll discuss later).

LEGAL FILINGS
Any and all legal transactions become your responsibility, including filing for copyright with the Library of Congress. A POD press will not offer you any legal protection, either.

SELLING RIGHTS
PODs will not attempt to sell any other versions of your book. This task lies in your court. However, you avoid having to give away a major chunk of any revenue generated from your book in this manner by doing it yourself.

CREDIBILITY
Even though self-publishing is becoming more and more common, POD books simply do not carry the same credibility as those published with a traditional house. This credibility issue can be wide-ranging—many media outlets will not review or promote self-published titles, and many bookstores will not carry them on their shelves.

However, book sales equate to reputations, and good reputations equate to credibility. So, the better job you do in creating a professional product and marketing it, the more book sales you will gain, and the more credibility you will be building for your "publishing house." Hardly anyone had heard of tiny Hampton Roads Press until they published Walsh's *Conversations with God*, which was eventually sold to a major house, who made it into a bestseller. Now, everyone in the publishing world knows of Hampton Roads as one of the finest New Age publishers in the business. All it takes is one big book.

LITERARY AGENTS

You don't need (nor do you have to compensate) a literary agent to land a deal with a self-publisher.

THE ADVANCE

Advances are not offered for self-published books.

EARNINGS

You will receive upwards of eight times as much money per book sold from the sale of a self-published book as opposed to what you would receive from a traditional publisher. For example, on a book that sells for $20, you can expect to receive between $2 and $3 in royalties, per book sold, from a conventional press, while a POD selling for the same amount would normally net you between $13 and $15.

Fees Associated with POD Publishing

Because almost every facet of the publishing process is your responsibility under the POD system, you will encounter fees to get certain tasks accomplished. For each option I'll discuss below, you could go a budget route or a high-end route—you'll need to decide what's best for your financial situation and the book. You can actually self-publish your POD book for as little as a few hundred dollars if you choose to do the vast majority of the labor yourself. But that assumes you're skilled in many areas of the process—formatting, design, legalese, and so on.

One of my students decided to do virtually everything herself when she self-published her novel. However, despite the depth of her idea, her drive, and her passionate prose, the book *looked* like she had handled all the tasks herself, and its dire need for editing took away from the eventual success of the story. So, I wouldn't recommend going this route—it's OK to hire experts to help you spread your passionate message to the world. Even though this student was able to clear her bottom line quickly, I strongly feel that her work lived a life far less than its potential. However, what you choose to do with each of the following options is completely up to you. Just make sure you can live with your choices while offering your literary baby the chance it deserves.

POD COMPANY FEES

You must pay a fee to have your book printed at a POD company. It's approximately $100 plus the price it costs to print your book, which is approximately $4 per paperback book and $8 to $10 for hardcover. This price is approximately 25 percent higher per book than you would expect to pay if you employed the past form of self-publishing. This is where a POD house makes its profit.

To see an accurate representation of your fees, multiply the printing costs per book type (hardcover, paperback) by the number of books you might print for promotional purposes. (These are not books you'd sell to others—the press will print copies based on actual orders received.)

EDITING

There are two main types of editing to think about for your book—a style edit, sometimes also called a line edit or developmental edit, and a copyedit. Here is more information about both.

Style Editing

Style editing usually comprises a "big picture" review of your manuscript. The editor will ensure that information appears in the proper order, makes sense, and is written clearly. Personally, because

I am a professional writer, I feel that a style editor is absolutely necessary. The suggestions of a good style editor can turn a good book into a great one. In fact, many a famous author owes much or his or her success to the suggestions and work of a great style editor. So I strongly suggest that you consider running your finished manuscript by any one of the great style editors that are available. Doing so is well worth the investment.

To find a good style editor, look in the *Literary Market Place* (also called the *LMP*, which is available in all libraries) for listings of editors. You can also look through the listings associated with The Author's Den portion of my website. Following are some ways to ensure you find an editor who's a good match for your work:

- Make sure when interviewing potential candidates that you request the references and examples of their work. Let your candidates also review a sampling of your work to see what suggestions they may have for improvement.
- As you go over your candidates' suggestions for improvement, pay very special attention to their objectivity. You want to ensure that you will be working with an objective editor and not a frustrated writer. If you use a frustrated writer, this person will attempt to rewrite your book for you in his or her style, as opposed to trying to aid you in bringing out your own voice.

Prices for a competent style editor vary *very* widely depending on the amount of work you need done, the length of your book, and how experienced your editor is. The cost can be as little as $800 or as much as $10,000.

Sedona Secret
USE THE *LMP*

You'll see that I recommend the *Literary Market Place* frequently—it really is the gold standard for publishing services. You can also visit *www. literarymarketplace.com* for an online database of their listings, which they offer for a weekly or annual fee.

Copyediting

Even if you are one of those people who somehow picked up the force-feeding of grammar, punctuation, and spelling in school, at some point you will become blind to a credible review of your own work. So, it is essential that you have your book copyedited by someone else—a professional—before handing it over to your formatter.

Again, the *Literary Market Place* (LMP), which is available at the library, is a highly recommended source for finding professional copyeditors. A reasonable cost for copyediting a book is $2 per Word page (assuming a double-spaced manuscript). You can find a list of copyeditors who I recommend on my website: *www.TomBird.com*.

FORMATTING

Formatting refers to the process of converting your manuscript (likely in a Word document) into a fully designed book. The person you hire for this task is by far the most important individual you will deal with. No matter how much work you put into your book, if you try to skimp here to save a few bucks, and the formatter you hire does a less-than-adequate job, your book will look terrible. As a result, your book sales will suffer, if not disappear altogether. Here are some tips for finding a good formatter:

- Make sure that your formatter has worked with the POD press you choose. If he or she has not, you may wind up paying for this person's education to learn how to do so.
- Ask to see examples of this person's work, and don't be shy about requesting a list of professional references.
- Let your potential formatters read some of your manuscript before signing on. Not only will this give you an idea of how sincere the person is, but doing so will also allow you to audit and compare any ideas they may have for formatting your book. This person needs to be not only technically sound and proven, but creative and artistic as well.
- Get potential formatters to quote you a flat fee for all the work on your project. That way, you avoid any hidden costs and you

aren't paying for foul-ups on their end (say, if their file isn't compatible with a printer's needs and they have to fix something technical).

Good formatters are hard to find, so start searching for this person as soon as possible. To find some formatters I recommend, check out my website, *www.TomBird.com*, or call printers in your area for recommendations. Depending upon the length of your book, how elaborate you want it to look, and the number of "elements" to be designed (does your book have boxes, quotes, charts, and so on?), formatting will cost you between $600 and $2,200. If that sounds like a lot of money to you, please keep in mind how important the presentation of your book is to your potential readers. And, be grateful that it's that cheap—remember, only a few years ago this service (via typesetting) would have cost you tens of thousands of dollars.

COVER DESIGN

Yes, you can do this yourself. However, there is a good chance that your potential readers will be able to tell. In that case, you will probably lose book sales. The first thing that a potential reader sees is the cover of your book. If it looks unprofessional or does not grab his or her attention, you lose a sale. It's that simple. Here are some tips for finding a qualified cover designer:

- Cover artists need to be creative, so don't be afraid to ask for a quick list of their ideas on your book cover before entering into any type of agreement.
- Ask for professional references and examples of previous covers the person has designed.
- Make sure that he or she is intimately familiar with meeting the technical demands of your POD house. Otherwise, you may end up paying for the education this person should already possess.
- Avoid, at all costs, web services whose prices seem cheaper than others but offer only a few "stock" styles of cover for you to

choose from. It is best and most professional looking if you have something individually created for your cover.

- Ask for a flat rate that includes all necessary work on your cover.

As with formatters, a good cover artist is hard to find. Check the *LMP* or my website, *www.TomBird.com*. Average costs for this service range from $600 to $900.

LEGAL PROTECTION

Since the POD press will offer you very few or no legal services, you'll probably need to undertake these filings on your own. Here are the three most important legal transactions you'll need to make.

Creating a Business Entity

You will need to form your own business entity to go the POD route, which can range anywhere in cost from $10 to $100. Don't be intimidated by this step. It is wise, for tax purposes and to receive additional legal protection, that you consider forming a separate legal entity to handle the publication of your book. Also, don't name your publishing house after yourself. That way, if you run into unexpected legal problems, your name doesn't become tarnished. I would also suggest that you at least run your chosen arrangement by a competent accountant or attorney. I routinely budget $250, which is normally more than enough to cover the cost of the review.

Copyrighting Your Book

You may also be responsible for copyrighting your material. When choosing your POD house, check into what services they offer. Do they handle the copyright of your material or do you? If you are responsible, you can complete the task online for approximately $35 through the Library of Congress. Your attorney can also handle it. With an attorney's fee included, it would cost several hundred dollars more than the $35 charged if you go directly through the Library of Congress.

Liability Review

If you would like an attorney to review your manuscript for any potentially dangerous statements or claims (a service normally provided by traditional publishing houses), you'll simply have to find a lawyer qualified to do so. They can be found by searching online or in the phone book for intellectual property attorneys.

MARKETING YOUR BOOK

Once, at an Intensive Retreat I was offering, Dick O'Connor, a longtime New York editor I had brought in to co-present, made a very interesting point. In trying to illustrate where our students should focus their promotional attention as authors, he drew a small dot in the middle of a flip chart.

"What is this?" he asked. After no one replied, Dick answered for them. "The number of Americans who read hardcover books."

Then he drew a small circle around the dot and asked, "What's this?" Again, no one dared to answer, so he replied for them a second time. "The number of people who read paperback books."

Then Dick drew a huge circle around the smaller circle, and asked for a third time, "What's this?" No longer waiting for a response, Dick replied quickly. "Those who don't read books at all."

The point I'm trying to make is that expensive, major media blanket advertising is a waste of time, especially for authors. There is a small, enthusiastic audience that you need to approach. After you've done that, you can do what any other publisher would do: rely on word-of-mouth to sell your book.

Getting Fiction Reviewed

If you are writing fiction, the best way to find that small, enthusiastic audience is through reviews written on your book. The three most influential reviewers in the industry are *Publishers Weekly* (*www.publishersweekly.com*), *Kirkus Reviews* (*www.kirkusreviews.com*), and *The Library Journal* (*www.libraryjournal.com*). Unfortunately, however, neither *Publishers Weekly* or *Kirkus Reviews* will review

POD or self-published works. Kirkus does have an arm called Kirkus Discoveries (*www.kirkusdiscoveries.com*) that will review self-published titles—but for a $400 fee. Each of these publications' websites tell you exactly what needs to be done to have your book considered for a review. Keep in mind, though, no matter who you ask to review your book, you must get it, even if it is in rough form, into their hands as far in advance of your planned publication date as possible. You want them to review it just before or at your publication date, so you need to allow them time to conduct the review.

The book *Guerrilla Publicity* (coauthored by renowned book publicist Rick Frishman) is a great resource for other places to send your book to be reviewed. I also suggest checking out the website *www.automaticbestseller.com*. Chris Guerrerio, the inspiration behind this site, sold more than a million copies of his own books on the Internet via an ingenious mixture of promotional plans and strategies, including getting book reviews done for cheap or, in some cases, for no money at all. His tips might help you out.

> "My first language was shy. It's only by having been thrust into the limelight that I have learned to cope with my shyness."
>
> Award-winning actor and Sedona resident Al Pacino

As far as other magazines, syndication services, and newspapers are concerned, their corporate names and addresses can be found in the *Literary Market Place* (LMP), again, which is usually available at libraries. Review their book review submission guidelines and try to call to get a book reviewer's name. You're more likely to get your book into the right hands if your package is addressed to a specific person. The costs to get your book reviewed are minimal—you'll just need to cover the expenses of creating review copies and mailing them.

Getting Nonfiction Publicized

Nonfiction works benefit from a potential audience from radio and television interviews. The most efficient route to gain access to every TV and radio interviewer throughout the country is through a publication entitled *Radio-Television Interview Reporter* (RTIR; *www.rtir.com*). *RTIR* compiles listings and descriptions of books and their authors and is sent out three times a month to every major and minor media source in the country—more than 21,000 media are contacted with each mailing!

RTIR is a fee-based service. It does, however, usually offer specials. You'll usually have to pay $1,200 per six-ad contract, which covers running your ad six times, and an array of other services and products as well, including a database of their entire media mailing list. Yes, $1,200 is a lot of money, but I still highly recommend the use of this service. The time and effort you would have to spend to contact 21,000 media outlets is simply astronomical and unrealistic. *RTIR*'s extensive website can answer all your questions.

Setting Up a Website

Yes, I know that it's possible to set up a website for under $50. The trouble with that site, though, is that it looks like a website that you set up for under $50. Because readers these days are very web-savvy, you need to have a professional website.

Scan the Internet for the websites of some of your favorite authors and take note of what they have done that you like. You can look on those pages to see if you can find the name of the person or company who designed the sites you like best and try to contact them to design your site. Or, ask for references from friends or colleagues. Follow the same procedures that you employed when acquiring the services of an editor, artist, or formatter:

- Ask for references and for them to offer you ideas on what they would do with your site. Ask for examples of their work as well.
- Accept only a flat, all-inclusive price as their bid to enable you to avoid the mystery and disappointment of the hourly rate.
- Make sure your webmaster has the abilities to upload materials, like your book cover, to major bookselling sites, such as Amazon .com and BarnesandNoble.com.

- Ask the designer about his experience in search engine optimization—which attunes your website to the liking of search engines, which will eventually lead to your popularity on the Internet. I have listed on my website, *www.TomBird.com*, the top webmaster, Search Engine Optimization (SEO) engineer I know. He can be found under the recommendations section.

You'll need to budget about $1,200 for your website, which will include the reservation of your website name, yearly fees, and your programmer's labor.

Use Rick Frishman's Expertise

I cannot even begin to cover all the marketing avenues your book could find. As I mentioned, to best understand all of the promotional opportunities available to you, read Rick Frishman's books *Guerrilla Publicity: Hundreds of Sure-Fire Tactics to Get Maximum Sales for Minimum Dollars* and *Guerrilla Marketing for Writers: 100 Weapons to Help You Sell Your Work*. Rick is the president of the largest and most influential book publicity firm in the world, Planned Television Arts (or PTA), and he is a marketing genius. Each book costs only $14.95, and they are worth their weight in gold. Read both books, take notes if you like, and then start implementing the valuable suggestions Rick makes. Choose what feels comfortable to you, leave the rest behind, and then keep promoting.

PTA also works out a special deal for my students as long as you are willing to do the majority of the legwork yourself. If you would like their direct assistance in promoting your book, they will design a professional promotional campaign for you and implement it over half a year for an average of $1,500 per month. Even though this may sound expensive, the services and instructions you will receive are comparable to what some traditional publishers pay three to four times as much for. The big difference is that you wind up doing the majority of the legwork, but the price is a very good investment, especially if you want to be a full-time author.

TOTALING UP YOUR FEES

Let's add up these fees so you have an idea of what it will cost you to publish a standard, 60,000-word paperback POD title.

POD company fees (printing 150 promo copies @ $4 each)	$600
Copyediting (~225 Word pages x $2/page)	$450
Formatting	$1,000
Cover design	$750
Legal transactions	$300
Basic marketing campaign	$1,000
Website creation	$1,200
Total	**$5,300**

Here are some add-ons you may want to consider:

Style editing	$3,000
Upscale marketing campaign	$3,000 per year
Total extras	**$6,000**

It's true that you'll need a decent amount of cash to go the POD route. If you're financially strapped, it simply may not be an option for you.

Choosing the Right POD House

Even though the POD industry is relatively new, it hasn't taken long for some unworthy alternatives to infiltrate it. Since there is no governing body of ethics in this industry to keep snakes from creeping in, it is up to you to discern for yourself who is right and wrong for you. Your decision should boil down to a few basic facts:

- **Turnaround time:** How quickly will the POD house be able to produce your book? Don't settle for anything more than thirty working days.

- **Background:** Ask for references and samples of books they have published. The amount of time they've been in business is also an important factor.
- **General costs:** How much do they charge and what can you expect for your fee?
- **Print cost:** How much will it cost to have your book printed?
- **Royalties:** A true POD house doesn't pay royalties to their authors because the authors are given 100 percent of all monies received for book sales. Yet, you'll find houses that refer to themselves as PODs yet proudly proclaim they pay their authors a whopping 25 percent royalty rate. Let me straighten this out for you. You pay for all the expenses to have your book edited and printed, and they don't provide any type of service at all in these cases. You write the book and you pay them to simply add it to their computer database. Then they profit from every book you have printed and they want to receive 75% of the monies from the sale of the book? For doing what? Do *not* use these companies.
- **Credibility:** At this juncture in their development, POD presses do not offer you any credibility. If someone from a POD house tells you that your association with their name does offer you credibility, run—don't walk—away from them.
- **Distribution channels:** Ingram is the finest and most accepted wholesale distributor of books. If a POD house that you are considering does not use them, ask why. No other distributor of books comes close to matching up.

Writer's
REFLECTION

Compile your potential POD presses' information, then rate each one in the categories listed from 1 to 10, with 10 being the highest rating. Then, since the topic of royalties and distribution are the two most important categories for long-term consideration, double whatever the score each POD alternative comes up with in those two areas. Then add up your totals. The highest score should be the right POD house for you.

E-Books

At the time of this writing, the concept of e-books is beginning to receive its due. By definition, e-books are simply electronic versions of books that can be sold and downloaded online and, because of their almost nonexistent production costs, generate a hefty profit for the author. E-books are also great because they can easily and efficiently, for no cost, be marketed throughout the world, via the Internet, within minutes.

So why hasn't this wave of potential swept the globe and taken over the publishing industry? Why, when the legendary author Stephen King tried to market his own books in this manner, did the concept prove to be a tremendous failure? Because Americans still want the bound book; it is simply what they have gotten used to receiving for their money. With the advent of electronic book readers (such as Amazon's Kindle and Sony's Reader), specifically designed to facilitate e-books, and a more savvy, computer-based readership entering the market, e-books have become more viable. I recently read an article about a brand-new novelist who sold over a million e-books of his first work, which, of course, led to a huge advance from a conventional publisher.

I would suggest converting your finished manuscript into an e-book as soon as possible. That way, you will have copies available for promotional use as well as for marketing on the Internet in an attempt to create a greater awareness of not only you as an author, but your book as well. Creating an e-book is quite simple and doesn't cost anything. To convert your manuscript to an e-book

Writer's
REFLECTION

Whew! We have covered a lot in this chapter. Take a deep breath. Then, before moving on to the next chapter, pull out your pad of lineless paper and pen, and do a circle drawing around the following topics:

1. What does publishing mean to me?

2. Is there anything that frightens me about publishing, and, if so, what?

3. What form of publishing or plan of publishing is my book calling out to me to follow?

simply translates to converting it into a PDF file. To do this, go to *www.adobe.com*. You will find (at the time of this writing) that Adobe allows you to convert up to five files (and your book in the digital world is nothing more than a file) to PDF for free.

To keep up with the latest breaking news and tips on this rapidly evolving trend, check out my website, *www.TomBird.com*.

Making the Right Decision for Your Book

Your book is like your literary child, and you want the best for it. How you offer this child to the public is where publishing comes in. Forget about the prestige and wealth that you may have inappropriately associated with publishing. All publishing is there to do is make available to the public whatever literary gift you may have. That's it. When looking at it from that perspective, choosing the right publishing option is really not much different than picking the right college or university to further a child's education. Review the information in this chapter, consider your financial status, think about how you want to share your book with the world, and make a decision that fits you best. No matter which way you pick, your valuable literary child will have found its way into the world—which is simply what publishing is there to provide and nothing more.

> "Raising kids is part joy and part guerrilla warfare."
>
> Acclaimed actor and frequent attendee of the Sedona Film Festival Ed Asner

Conclusion

Never before has the world of publishing provided so many wonderful alternatives for an author not only to get his/her work out to the world but to get paid more than handsomely for doing so. Don't rush into this decision—weigh your options carefully.

"Always remember that this whole thing started with a dream and a mouse."

Frequent visitor to Sedona, Walt Disney

"If everything isn't black and white, I say, 'Why the hell not?'"

Actor and former Sedona resident John Wayne

chapter nine

Writing an Effective
Query Letter

LET'S SAY THAT it's Christmas Day or Hanukkah. You've taken weeks to prepare a spread that should grace the cover of *Holiday Meals Magazine*. Everyone is there—dozens of close friends and family who have come in from all across the globe. You are just about to proudly present the food to your cherished, famished herd, when the doorbell rings. Thinking that it may be a late-arriving guest, you rush over, open the door, and find me, whom you have never seen before, standing there.

Expecting Uncle Hank, Aunt Vi, or someone else you love and adore to be making a last-minute, surprise appearance, you are caught completely off guard by me, the stranger at the door. As a result, you don't really know what to say.

"Ah, yes," you mumble under your breath, "may I help you?"

"Yes," I reply, as cocky and confident as can be. "I would like you to leave with me immediately to do fifty hours of free, physical labor."

You don't know what to say, but you're sure as heck that you don't want to go. So, you pull back, utter a few polite apologies, and softly close the door in my face.

What does a scenario such as this have to do with your publishing aspirations?

Everything.

You see, when you follow the procedure most new writers use, you're forcing an editor to be that person cooking dinner. Your book is me, standing at the door, unrequested and requiring work. The last thing that an editor or literary agent wants to see appear on his or her desk is an unrequested, full-length manuscript from an unrecognized, new author. The reality is that there is barely time for editors and agents to read the books that they are contractually obligated to review, let alone others.

The Simple Truth: You Need a Query Letter

Many aspiring authors make the mistake of sending their hard-earned manuscript off to a publishing house without first sending a query letter. When they do so, the publisher will almost certainly reject it. Unbeknownst to the author, their rejection springs not from the lack of quality of their work, but instead from violating the simple but essential, unwritten etiquette of the literary world. They did not send a query letter.

Let's frame this situation in a real-life context. If you wanted to land a job with a respected company, you couldn't expect much, if any, success if you just walked into their headquarters and demanded a high-ranking, executive position (or any other job, for that matter). You would be lucky just to be thrown out onto the street. Wouldn't it make sense that if you were to emulate the same action in the literary

COPYRIGHTING

Many students ask me how they can protect their work from being stolen. First, know that you cannot copyright an idea. This means that if you submit a query letter for review, you can only copyright the query letter and not the idea that it represents. So, what do you do? Simple—protect anything you've written. Copyright your book (perhaps with the assistance of an attorney) through the Library of Congress. Doing it yourself will cost you around $35. Visit *www.copyright.gov/register* to get all the appropriate registration forms. Of course, if you go through an attorney, you will have to pay legal fees.

arena by firing off your manuscript to a publishing house without first going through the proper channels that you would meet with the same results? Of course. So to dodge such an unnecessary rejection, you should follow a system comparable to the one utilized in the job placement field.

In most cases, when you apply for a job you are expected to submit a personal letter and résumé. The literary arena has its own version of that as well—the query letter. However, in the literary marketplace, rarely is its version sent directly to potential publishers. Because of the usually high traffic volume, it is instead sent to an essential middleman who fills the same role as a headhunter or job placement counselor, called a literary agent. Just as a résumé secures a job interview, the query letter secures a literary interview with an editor or agent for your work.

Pearl of *Wisdom*

This point is important enough to be made again: A query letter doesn't sell one's work; it simply gives a writer the opportunity he or she needs to sell his or her work. That's all.

Using a query letter greatly increases your chance of a sale. Ignoring it vastly increases your chance of failure. If you've been impatiently saying, "To hell with the query letter," and contemplating submitting the manuscript you've written instead, don't do it. No matter how good your material is, you'll only be setting yourself up for failure. Let's look at some other benefits of using a query letter to find a literary agent.

The Query Letter Allows You to Gauge the Depth of Potential Interest in Your Project

If you send out a query letter and find there is enough interest in your project to devote your time, energy, and, potentially, money to it, great! If there isn't much or any interest, the query letter can save you from wasting any further resources. On the other hand, positive responses to your query letter build confidence in your project and your approach to your writing. This added confidence will show itself in your writing style, and also in the savvy with which you approach the publishing of your material.

The Query Letter Package Prevents Creative Constipation

That's right, creative constipation. If you're anything like me, and I have to believe that you are, ideas are probably flowing through your mind all the time. If you don't find some way to release them, they'll get backed up. As a result, you'll lose your ability to identify what your creative mind is trying to share with you because you have too many ideas trapped up there. You'll get frustrated and angry. And you can't write well from a place of frustration and anger, so your DWW will be cautious in its future attempts to communicate with you. That, of course, is not what you want—you want your DWW to have a free and clear connection to you at all times.

By properly utilizing a query letter, which is relatively easy to write once you get the hang of it, you will be putting those ideas to use, freeing yourself of the dreaded creative constipation.

Sending a Query Letter Package Is *Fun*

No, I'm not crazy. Think of it in these terms: There is no pressure involved. If whomever you contact likes your idea, great! If no one appears to like your idea, you can send your query letter elsewhere or change the idea slightly. Just be sure you're always writing what you feel passionate about. Besides a small amount of your time, a little work on the Internet, a few stamps, a bit of stationery, and a few envelopes, you don't have much to lose.

The Two Types of Query Letters

You will either send a query letter for fiction (even if you can't factually account for 1 percent of your manuscript, it is still seen as fiction) or nonfiction. There are no special considerations for different genres within those broad categories. What you are writing is either fiction or nonfiction, period. Though both the fiction and nonfiction query letters are made up of five separate parts, each one has its own unique design.

Here are some general tips to keep in mind for both fiction and nonfiction query letters:

- The query should always be neatly typed.
- Limit the query to *one page* in length.
- Limit the size of your paragraphs, giving the letter the appearance of a quick, easy read.
- Include your name, address, and telephone number.

Those are the undisputable ground rules. Here are more specific techniques for fiction and nonfiction query letters.

Five Elements of a Fiction Query Letter

Here are the five sections to include in your query letter.

1. THE TITLE

Most new writers erroneously spend far too much time choosing a title for their project. They innocently believe that whatever title they commit to in their query letter will eventually become the title of their book, which is more than likely not true. In fact, it is not unusual for a title to change several times before a final choice is made. Professionals in the literary business are well aware of this, so they won't hold you to any of your initial impulses.

DOTTING YOUR I'S

Personalize your query letter by adding the name of the literary agent and agency, or editor and publisher. Sign it at the bottom in your usual manner and promise to provide anyone interested in seeing more material with whatever they request.

For the purpose of a query letter, it is essential that the title merely attract a reader's interest and be representative of something in your work. That's all. Just come up with something that will grab your potential reader's attention.

2. THE GRABBER

The Grabber comprises the first paragraph of a fictional query letter. It should be no more than three short sentences in length. Its purpose is to further entice the reader to review the remainder of your query. No matter how good the middle or end of your query letter may be, if you lose an editor or agent here, she won't read the rest. Your work will thus be returned to you without ever having gotten a fair chance to be seen.

Here are three suggestions for writing an effective Grabber:

- **Don't begin with a question.** Your readers simply won't know enough about your characters or your story in general to care about the answer to your question.
- **Appeal to as many of the reader's five senses as possible.** The key to effective fiction is to get your readers to feel. Thus, the best way to grab their attention is to appeal to their senses. Create an interesting image for your readers to get lost in, and you will have them hooked.
- **Make a positive comparison.** To give your readers a better idea of the potential of your work, compare the eventual success of your proposed project with a literary success. For example, "What Margaret Mitchell's *Gone with the Wind* Did for Rhett Butler, my novel *Something About Harry* will do for Hank Fisher." This technique is very successful, so spend days if necessary to find one that will work for your book. That's how important this aspect is to an effective query letter.

3. THE MAIN CHARACTERS

Before you can share any plot details with your agent, editor, or publisher, it is essential that you first identify your top two or three characters (one paragraph devoted to each). Your goal with each character description is to create the proper imagery to bring the character to life in your reader's mind, and to begin to gently introduce your storyline or plot.

4. THE PLOT OR STORYLINE

Use the next portion of your query (three or four paragraphs) to share your plot or storyline with the reader.

5. THE ENDING

Use the last paragraph to leave your prospective audience with something to remember you and/or your project by. Try reiteration the information you used to grab their attention in the first paragraph.

Check out Appendix B for sample query letters.

Five Elements of a Nonfiction Query Letter

Here are the specific sections you'll need for a nonfiction (or poetry) query letter.

1. THE TITLE

The purpose of the title in a nonfiction query letter is exactly the same as its fictional counterpart. It is meant to attract attention. It need not necessarily be considered your final title. In fact, what you choose as your title at this stage will probably change several times before your work appears in print. So, don't place undue pressure upon yourself by sweating over a title. Come up with something appropriate that attracts a reader's attention and go with that.

2. THE GRABBER

Catch your reader's attention with a comparison-evoking statement, in the same manner as the fictional query letter. For example, "My book *All About Apples* will do for the orchard industry what Tom Peters's book *In Search of Excellence* did for business."

3. AN EXPLANATION OF THE BOOK'S MARKET

The key to a nonfiction query letter is to identify a significant population who would be interested in reading your work. You'll need to describe that audience in some detail and explain how large it is. Besides your primary audience, list any ancillary audiences you think would be interested in reading about your topic.

In addition, you need to identify what void in the literary world you will be filling with your project. How is your book different from others like it? What does it offer that its competition does not? Be sure to do your homework and know your category's bestsellers. The literary agent or publisher will certainly know your book's competition, and so should you. The more benefits your book provides, the better. You don't need to delve into great detail (after all, the query letter should be only one page) but mention the highlights.

4. THE MAKEUP AND DESIGN OF YOUR PROJECT

This is where you give agents, editors, and publishers a quick but enlightening rundown of some of the chapter headings, sectional breakdowns, and topics to be covered in your work. You should also mention any important elements you plan to include—for example, nutritional information (the amount calories, fat, and so on) for each recipe in a cookbook.

5. THE ENDING

As with the fictional query letter, leave your readers with something favorable by which to remember you and/or your project.

Check out Appendix B for sample query letters.

Sedona Secret
KEEP YOUR CREDENTIALS IN CHECK

Don't jam up your query letter with a long list of credits, degrees, and credentials, if you have any. Simply list any pertinent degrees in your letterhead and quickly mention any credits or credentials in no more than a sentence or two at the conclusion of your letter.

Query Letters for Articles, Short Stories, and Poetry

Since most literary agents do not represent articles, short stories, and poetry, it is common practice to submit your query letter directly to the editor of a publication. In some cases, the magazine (or publisher you are approaching), may have on staff a submissions or acquisitions editor or a specialty editor who would be in charge of reviewing your type of material. If that's true, send your material to that person.

Pearl of *Wisdom*

It's still a good idea to send query letters, even if a particular magazine only accepts completed work. Doing so will enable you to gauge your source's reaction to your ideas and then modify and appropriately adjust your work before submitting it for review. Thus, sending your query letter first will increase your chance of an eventual sale.

Finding Places to Get Articles and Short Stories Published

Where can you find a listing of sources that you can approach with your ideas for a magazine article or short story? Here are a few suggestions:

- **Newsstand:** This is the best place to go when researching possible homes for your article and short story ideas. Not only can you catch a glimpse of the publication or publications you will be approaching, but you can also copy down the correct name and address of the appropriate contact in each case. In a business with a high turnover rate like the magazine field, this is a necessity.
- ***Writer's Digest* magazine by Writer's Digest Books:** This publication boasts hundreds of potential sources for your work. However, because of the high turnover rate of editors, be sure to double-

check any information with a newsstand issue of the magazine you're considering, or visit *www.writersdigest.com.*

- *The Writer's Handbook* by The Writer Inc.: This publication provides a smaller listing than *Writer's Market.*

Writer's
REFLECTION

Time to do more circle drawings, which will enable you to release any unnecessary fear or resistance you may feel around everything associated with the query letter. Use the following statements as starting points:

1. Query letters are my friends.
2. What can a query letter do for me both professionally and personally?

Submitting Queries for Magazine Articles, Short Stories, or Poetry

As with books, it is essential to utilize a multiple submissions system. Here's a two-step process:

1. First, arrange your potential sources from who would pay you the most for a prospective piece to who would pay you the least. If you don't know what a specific publication would pay you, call and ask them, use a SASE to send for a copy of their writers' guidelines, or visit their websites. Calling is quicker, but occasionally you may find yourself caught in an awkward position by doing so because you may end up turning down a sincerely nice publication because they can't pay you enough.

2. After you've properly arranged your sources, send to a few of the top-paying sources first, giving them at least four weeks to respond. Then send to the next highest-paying group, allowing them the same amount of time to reply, before approaching your remaining sources.

Why do you go to your best-paying sources first? The answer is simple. You want to allow the sources that can offer you the most money, as well as the highest degree of exposure (the two usually go hand in hand), the first opportunity to publish your work. By starting at the bottom, you may be selling yourself short by potentially keeping your work from being published by a much better-paying source.

Exercise: Write Your Query Letter

Now that you're armed with the background information you need and have read some successful samples, go ahead and write a draft of your query letter during your writing session. Follow the Three Rs of Writing and connect with your DWW, as always.

Conclusion

Once you have mastered the query letter, you have paved the way of your route into the wild and wonderful world of conventional publishing.

"The more you are like yourself, the less you are like anyone else, which makes you unique."

Frequent visitor to Sedona, Walt Disney

"It's exceeded my expectations, in every way, really. The people are nicer than I imagined they could have been. They were more supportive of me than I hoped they would be."

Frequent visitor of the Sedona Film Festival and actor Rick Schroeder

chapter ten

Choosing a Literary Agent, Part I

THE GOOD NEWS is that there are thousands of literary agents. The bad news is that even though there are a few governing bodies that attempt to do so, there is no universally accepted ethical body (like the American Medical Association for the medical field) that determines who is and who is not qualified to be a literary agent. What this means, in my estimation, is that more than 75 percent of those individuals who call themselves literary agents fall way short of the title, or in the worst cases, are downright frauds.

How Can You Tell the Good from the Bad?

One way is to find out how and when they make their money. Literary agents are commission-based salespeople, so they shouldn't make any money until you get a book deal. An agent also:

- Has the expertise to help you edit and refine your writing for submission to publishing houses.
- Fills the role of literary legal counsel and negotiates and enforces your literary contracts.

How do you know whether an agent is a potential fraud? Quite simply, if they charge extra fees above and beyond their 15 percent cut for those two services, be very leery.

Let's take that point a little further. Let us say that a prospective agent, Bob, has expressed an interest in reviewing your manuscript for potential representation to a publisher. Bob reminds you, "Don't forget to send along the $1,200 reading fee with your manuscript."

Many so-called literary agents charge reading fees. No, that fee does not go to an outside service to review your material, but instead supplements the agent's income because he is not making enough money selling works to publishers. What does that tell you about Bob's ability as a literary salesperson? It's not very good. He certainly is not the type of person you want handling your literary gem.

The same goes with editing fees. These fees rose in popularity in the latter part of the last century in the literary industry, when authors began avoiding agents who charged a reading fee. A new group of "editing services" struck up mutually beneficially deals with agencies. All these agencies had to do was recommend the editing service to authors. If a referral from one of the agencies signed on with the editorial firm, the agency was given a 30 to 40 percent kickback from the fees charged by the editing service.

> "It's fun to dream the impossible."
>
> Frequent visitor to Sedona,
> Walt Disney

Pretty sweet deal, huh? For the unethical agency and editing service, maybe—but not for the innocent writer who in most cases was led to believe, by the agency, that all that was needed to achieve publication was one good, thorough edit. Unfortunately, even if that were the case, these firms couldn't have helped because they often employed inexperienced high school seniors and college underclassmen to revise and edit the manuscripts.

The rest of this chapter will give you tips and techniques for avoiding the agents who use these underhanded tactics.

Where to Find *Good* Agents

There are plenty of listings of literary agents available. Here are a few of the most thorough and reputable:

- **The *Literary Marketplace* (LMP):** The "Directory of the American Book Publishing Industry," as it is referred to by its publisher, can be found in almost any library, or online at *www.literarymarket place.com*. Though it offers the names, addresses, and telephone numbers, as well as a small description of approximately 400 literary agents, the majority of the information on each literary agent is meant for use by proven professionals within the field. Thus, the descriptions are often of little use to the new writer because they are so short and general in nature, and thus don't always offer the in-depth insight most new authors look for.
- ***Writer's Market*:** A book that is updated annually and offers a long listing of agents, and also a website (*www.writersmarket .com*) that offers news and advice from industry insiders, and the ability to manage and track your manuscript submissions.
- **Publishersmarketplace.com:** Offers in-depth descriptions on dozens of the top agencies as well as information about some of the best book editors, publicists, and so on. The cost is $20 a month to subscribe, which includes a daily newsletter e-mailed out to you. It's an invaluable and highly recommended source.
- **Mediabistro.com:** Offers many in-depth descriptions of literary agents, editors, and others. The cost to subscribe is approximately $250 a year. Also a highly recommended source.
- ***Jeff Herman's Guide to Literary Agents, Editors and Publishers*:** Updated every few years and offers a long listing of agents, editors, and publishers.
- **Independent listings:** Libraries often carry general listings of literary agents that have been published over the years. But oftentimes the addresses and telephone numbers listed in such publications are outdated, so check carefully. There are also a variety of Internet sources of this type available.

- **Tom Bird's Selective Guide to Literary Agents Database:** This is a database that I developed specifically new authors. It boasts a listing of more than 2,200 top literary agents who don't charge fees and who are open to accepting new clients. For your convenience and in an effort to save you time and money, it's only offered in electronic form. Find more information on it on my website, *www.TomBird.com*, or by calling my office at 928-203-0265.

How to Narrow Down Your Options

The acquisition of the proper literary representative is paramount to your success in this field. Allow me to stress again: find the right literary agent for *you*. Each literary agent is different. Each one has different qualities, likes, dislikes, and approaches. As with any partnership, the right literary agent will make you while the wrong one can break you. Thus, it is important not to just take the first literary agent that happens along and offers you representation. Base your decision on a significant amount of comparative research.

To evaluate a literary agent for possible contact, you should consider each of the following:

- **Area of expertise:** Do they handle the type of material you want to write?
- **Are they taking on new clients?** If they are not willing to take on anyone new, there's no reason to contact them.
- **Versatility:** How many different types of books a literary agent represents is very important. For example, if you choose an agent who only works with romance novels, and after he or she sells your first Harlequin you get an impulse to write a cookbook, you will have to go outside your present agent for representation.
- **Contacts:** Does the agents you are considering have developed contacts at the major publishing houses?
- **Commission rate:** What commission rate do they charge? (It should be 10 or 15 percent)

- **Clout:** Do they represent important writers so publishers pay attention to them? What new clients do they represent?
- **Sales ratio:** This information is hard to come by, but if you can acquire it, it will prove the most beneficial of all criteria considered. A sales ratio for a literary agent is simply the number of books sold per year per client. If a literary agent has 30 clients and sold 15 books last year, he or she averages one-half of a book sale per year per client represented, which is an outstanding ratio.
- **Size:** Small literary agents, with fifty clients or fewer, are oftentimes new in the business, hungrier, and willing to offer you more of their time than larger agents, who represent 150 clients or more. But keep in mind that larger, older, and, thus, more established agents usually have an inside track.
- **Personality:** Clearly, you want to get along with your agent and trust his or her judgment. Make sure that you strongly consider this when shopping for an agent.

A Step-By-Step Approach to Picking "The One"

Here is how to pick the agent that best suits your needs.

Step One: Make a List of 200 Agents

Go to one (or more than one) of the listings of literary agents mentioned earlier in this chapter. Then, based upon the criteria that is most important to you, choose at least 200 agencies that you feel,

Sedona Secret
CHECK AN AGENT'S LOCATION

Don't forget to consider an agent's location. To have a profitable working relationship with a literary agent, it is important that you are able to communicate easily. Sometimes, this means meeting in person. In addition, a specific location oftentimes indicates a person's attitude and approach to life or even their specialty.

for one reason or another, would be valid representatives for you. Remember, it's essential to be thorough, so more is better. After you've compiled a list of 200+, read their descriptions, and using your gut instincts, arrange your list in order from the literary agent you think would be best for you to the one you feel would be the least best for you.

Step Two: Send a Query Letter

Next, send your query letter to your entire listing at the same time. Don't be concerned that you are submitting to so many agents at the same time. If you were looking for a new job, you wouldn't send your resume out to one potential employer at a time, would you?

If any of the agents claim that they will not read multiply submitted query letters or that they want a listing of who else has received your query before reading it, take him or her off your list. The same goes for those who ask for an exclusive review of your manuscript. Can you imagine a potential employer telling you that he or she would not interview you unless you were not interviewing with others? Not only are suggestions such as those reflections of what is clearly an unfair labor practice, but they also bespeak of blatant insecurity.

Pearl of *Wisdom*

Remember, it's okay to send out your query letter before you have completed your book. In fact, I suggest doing so because the positive replies that you will receive will rid you of many of the fears that have plagued your efforts up to this point. Don't worry, none of the agents who will be interested in your work will have to see it immediately. They'll all still be around when your book is complete. When you do eventually submit your material to them for review, just include, to jog their memories, a copy of their original e-mail or letter back to you.

It's now time to decide which one of two potential methods you will employ to submit your query letter package.

VIA SNAIL MAIL

This option translates to addressing each of your 200 or more letters, labeling them, stuffing them, and purchasing both mailing postage and return postage for each source chosen. So, not only is it monetarily expensive, but it could take dozens of hours to complete as well. Going the snail mail route, with return postage included, will cost you $200 to send out 200 queries. It will take you an average of six to eight weeks before you can count on having received the majority of your replies.

ELECTRONICALLY

Up until just a few months after 9/11, that was about your only alternative. But at that point, something changed in the psyches of literary agents everywhere. In greater numbers than ever before, agents became open to accepting e-mailed query letter packages. Even though I was thrilled, I was still a bit skeptical. So, I e-mailed several query letters to ensure that this trend was indeed real and here to stay. To my amazement, not only was the percentage of positive replies nearly eight times higher than what I would have normally expected to receive via snail-mailed versions, but on an average more than 60 percent of those contacted replied within forty-eight hours.

So, your choice is really clear-cut. Choosing your literary agents from a database and e-mailing them out takes about twenty minutes, as opposed to an average of eighteen to twenty hours via the snail-mail route. Outside the purchase of the database listing (and you would have to acquire some sort of listing for the snail-mail route as well), it costs absolutely nothing to mail out your 200+ queries. You'll begin receiving responses within hours via the e-mail alternative and will have the vast majority of your replies back in your hands in days.

Now, I realize that some of you still do not feel comfortable using a computer, let alone the Internet. But the e-mail alternative is so much faster, more efficient, cheaper, and more successful that you must be able to use it. If you don't yet feel comfortable with your computer or the Internet, why not have a friend or a family member who is a bit more cyber-savvy submit your package for you? In the meantime, you can take a class at a local community center to become more acclimated.

Step Three: Wait.

After you've received your first offer to review, the next step is to sit back and collect acceptances, or work on another query letter (in a noncompeting field) for another book. There's nothing else that can be done until you have heard, whether they replied affirmatively or not, from at least 50 percent of your candidates. If, after ten days, you have yet to hear from certain agents, you can resubmit your query letter to them.

The Responses You Can Expect from Literary Agents

If you've followed my advice thus far, you won't receive any cruel, hurtful rejections from literary agents. That doesn't mean that every literary agent will want to see more of your book, it just means that you won't receive any of the harsh rejections of one's character or abilities you may have heard of your friends receiving, or that you may have even heard yourself. The reason for that is simple: you are projecting yourself professionally and following the unwritten etiquette of the industry.

What you *can* expect to receive are positive replies to your query letters. Positive replies will indicate a request for you to send a submission package, some sample material from your manuscript, or your entire book.

How many responses can you expect? Approximately 50 percent of the agents you query will respond within ten days. So if you queried 200 literary agents, you can expect to hear from about 100 of those within a week and a half. Of those replying, how many can you expect to respond positively? Since the income of these representatives is commissioned-based, they have to be very selective in who they take on as clients. With that said, approximately a 4 percent rate of positive replies would be considered excellent, which means if you heard back from 100 agents, you could expect four to reply positively to your query.

To substantially increase this number, I strongly suggest sending your query to as many agents as possible. For example, my selective guide to literary agents would allow you to submit to upward of a thousand agents or more if you were writing adult fiction or nonfiction. *Remember:* You only need to land *one* agent. More importantly, it is essential that he or she is the "right" agent. You can see some actual replies from literary agents in Appendix C.

the divine writer
within

Even with the economy down at the time of this writing, offers to new authors are up. How do I know that? My students send out an average of half a million query letters a year. Through their efforts, I receive an amazingly accurate cross-section of just what is and is not happening in publishing.

With the economy at its lowest point since the Great Depression, and the value of the book publishing industry dropping like a rock as well, I assumed that positive replies to query letter submissions would be substantially down as well. As a result, I was really, really, pleasantly surprised when I was dead wrong. In fact, in my twenty-five-plus years of monitoring the book publishing world, I had never seen a hotter or more prosperous time for new authors. In fact, many of my students received more than fifty positive replies from literary agents, and a few hauled in nearly ninety (both figures had been relatively unheard of).

The key to this trend lay in the fact that, in response to the economic slowdown, publishing houses, even though they were routinely shrinking their staff and laying off editors, needed to be even more aggressive, out of desperation to save their houses from going under, in pursuing new authors.

Don't Be Afraid

I discovered soon after beginning my work with aspiring authors that:

1. The only one person holding them back from succeeding in the wonderful world of book publishing and writing was the writer him/herself.
2. The fear that holds more authors back from succeeding than any other is the fear of *success.*

As outrageous as that may sound, it's true. I discovered that what aspiring authors feared most was exposure and change. In the case of even a so-called "good" change, the status quo of a writer's life shifts away from whatever situation he or she has been familiar with. And no matter how unpleasant the familiar situation was, the writer's LCB still equated it with security.

In addition, most aspiring authors have spent the majority of their lives hiding their real opinions and their genuine selves. As a result, they often-times subconsciously fear publication because it exposes the soft, sensitive, expressive, honest sides of themselves that they have been conditioned to keep hidden from the public view.

In response, most aspiring authors, despite all of the wonderful, life-changing things that the proper conception and submission of a query let-

Writer's
REFLECTION

Let's remove fears of success. Get out your large pad of lineless paper and pen, and do a circle drawing around the statement, "Why both the writing and submission of my query letter scares me." Your fears will expose themselves. In most cases, you will either find them to be different than you had expected them to be or less daunting than you anticipated. When you have nothing left to write, take a long look at them, and then crinkle up the pages and either throw them away or burn them. Conclude by doing two circle drawings around the following statements: "Why I will succeed as a writer" and "Why publication is great for me."

ter can do for them, fear greatly both the act of writing it and, most of all, submitting it. If you find yourself experiencing anxiety or fear about this, review the contract you made with yourself. Revisiting your goals will help remind you of your passion to spread your DWW's message with the world. If necessary, talk with some of the unconditional supporters who have a copy of your contract. Tell them about your fears and let them assure your LCB that you deserve the success you're about to achieve.

Conclusion

Now that you've written and submitted your query letter, you're well on your way to finding proper literary representation. You're very close to your goal of sharing your work with the world.

"You see much more of your children once they leave home."

Acclaimed actor and frequent attendee of the Sedona
Film Festival Ed Asner

"We're born alone, we live alone, we
die alone. Only through our love and
friendship can we create the illusion for a
moment that we're not alone."

Former Sedona resident and acclaimed filmmaker
and actor Orson Wells

chapter eleven

Choosing a Literary Agent, Part II

HERE ARE IMPORTANT things to keep in mind about this stage:

1. It could take anywhere from a few days to several months for an agent to review your material and get back to you.
2. Because of the number of submission packages agents receive, you should follow up with a courtesy phone call to ensure that your material was received.

This part of the process can be difficult for an excited, passionate writer, but you need to be patient.

Reviewing and Rating Your Agent Responses

If you have sent out your query letter packages and you have begun receiving responses, you probably already understand just how creatively schizophrenic this industry is.

First, your sources replied in a wide variety of ways—ranging from an e-mail, neatly typed letter, or polite telephone call (know that telephone calls are very rare and should be taken as a sign directly from God) to sloppily handwritten notes.

Second, they are probably far from what you expected them to be.

It is important to pay very close attention to your immediate reaction to each response, as this will serve as a true and accurate key to help you better understand exactly what type of person and/or agency your literary soul is leading you to, or away from. So, budget some time in a very relaxed space to look over your acceptances. While doing this, on a separate piece of paper, list each agency offering an acceptance (I offer a system for doing this is in my Selective Guide to Literary Agents database).

Then rate your agents, giving each a score from a low of 1 to a high of 10, based on two factors: their enthusiasm for your work, and how strongly you feel about each one. Add those two figures together. The sum you come up with will allow you to rank them from whom you like best to whom you like least.

The Submission Package

Before we go further, let's talk about your submission package(s). No matter what shape, size, or design it takes, you'll put it together after receiving positive replies to your query letter from a literary agent. If he or she is interested in your work after reviewing your submission package, there is a good chance that you will be offered a contract. Once that happens, your agent will help you refine your submission package to attract publishers. After that is completed, it is sent off for sale. So, there are two versions of a submission package:

1. The version you send to literary agents
2. The version your agent helped you polish that you will send to publishers—often called the "proposal"

Sedona Secret
CHECK AN AGENT'S LOCATION

For an even more elaborate study of what a Proposal Package is and what it should look like, I strongly suggest reading a copy of Michael Larsen's *How to Write a Book Proposal*.

Writing a Book Proposal

Your book proposal is a more thorough look into your project. Nonfiction works also use the book proposal to explain ideas or concepts that many people may not know of. This introduction is spread throughout the sections of the proposal. Here are the main sections of a nonfiction proposal:

1. A title page
2. A table of contents
3. A one-page bio on the author (or a curriculum vitae)
4. An overview, giving a general idea of what is being proposed and why
5. The market
6. A chapter-by-chapter sketch of the book
7. An analysis of the book's competition and why this work is better and different
8. A collection of sample work from the book

Following are more elaborate descriptions of these elements.

Title Page
This should include the working title of your book, a designation that it's nonfiction, your name, address, phone number, and e-mail address.

Table of Contents
This is the table of contents for your proposal, not for your book. It will look like the eight-point list you just read.

Author Bio
The purpose of the one-page bio is to introduce the author (or authors) of the proposed work to a literary agent and publisher. To successfully compose a bio, follow the instructions on the following page.

- Identify what attributes make you the best writer *for this piece*.
- List any writing credentials or experiences that convey some authority in the field you are writing about. If you don't have credentials or experience, at least illustrate the significant commitment that you have made to the art of writing, even if that means just having kept a journal for the last twenty years.
- Specify the direction of your future interests.

It is usually best to organize these three points into separate paragraphs. Use the third person rather than first person—it is much easier to cover large amounts of ground quicker in that manner. It is also essential that the bio you write displays your style and character. Don't try to copy anybody. Cheap imitations never sell in the literary world. Be yourself, and let them see who you are.

The Overview

The book overview used for nonfiction is composed of the same five components that make up a query letter (see page 131). In essence, it is a long, long query letter designed to entertainingly answer all questions that a literary agent could potentially ask. You must approach and expound upon several topics, most of which you've already thought about for the query letter. They can be conveniently converted for use in your book overview. They are:

1. What is your idea for a book?
2. Who is your audience?
3. Why will your book be a valuable asset to your audience?
4. What do you hope to accomplish with the writing of your book?
5. What ideas do you have for the potential sale and promotion of the book?
6. How many words do you expect the book to be?
7. What are you willing to do to participate in the promotion of the book?
8. How long will it take you to complete the writing of the book?

Examples of an overview for your review are included in the sample proposal packages in Appendix D.

Market

In your opinion, who is going to purchase your book? Who makes up your primary audience? Your secondary audience? List them as specifically as possible—include gender, age, income levels, familial status, interests, location, and so on.

Competition

In this section, you'll compare the potential of your book with other books that have been published on the same subject. To do this, start out by making a broad general statement in regard to how your book compares, such as: "The following twelve books have been published in the last ten years on the same subject I will be addressing in my book, proving that there is a market for the work I am proposing. Where my book varies greatly from the following works is that: 1) my work is up to date; 2) my work offers greater reader interaction through quizzes, exercises, and assignments, a must in today's proactive world; and 3) it is far more in-depth than any of the other works."

Follow up your opening statement to this section with a quick one- or two-sentence description of each work along with a listing of not only the title and author's name of each book, but its copyright date, publisher, whether it was initially printed in hardcover or paperback, and price. Be sure to highlight in depth how your book stands out against each competitor.

The Chapter-by-Chapter Sketch

The chapter-by-chapter sketch gives a literary agent a more detailed idea of how your book will be composed. The main focus of the chapter-by-chapter sketch is to give your reader a deeper understanding of the content of each chapter without telling so much that it winds up boring him or her.

Sample Work

No matter what you've offered literary agents up to this point in your submission package, this section spells make-or-break time. There are two things that a literary agent will look for in any sample chapters you include:

1. How quickly you grab your reader's attention
2. How effectively you communicate and carry your story forward.

The Submission Package for Adult Fiction

The following must be included in a submission package for a book of adult fiction:

1. A title page
2. A table of contents
3. A synopsis
4. A chapter-by-chapter sketch
5. An author bio or curriculum vitae
6. Sample material

As you can see, most of the parts are the same as the nonfiction proposal, which I just detailed. The main difference is the synopsis.

Synoposis

Like the overview, the synopsis, which is employed for fiction, is a long query letter. Your synopsis must achieve two goals:

1. **It must carry the tone and creative tension of your book.** To do this, simply expand the thoroughly shortened storyline or plot, the fourth component, that you shared in your query letter (see page 131). Remember, use the reader's five senses to make your tale come to life.

2. **It must effectively address** the topics just listed for the overview. The difference is that you don't need to talk about them as directly as you do in an overview. Just let them come to life. Because of the enhanced length of this section, you can just blend them in with an opening description of your story.

A sample synopsis follows:

Places the Dead Call Home
By Paul L. Hall

Synopsis

On a summer night in 1958, bullets tear through the body of a young man on a lonely Oklahoma highway. Nineteen years later, a soldier lies in the pool of his own blood on an army base in Virginia. Death has made room at home for both of them. Death can always find room for more.

Josh Kincaid is a common link to both events. In 2002, when Kincaid's cousin proposes an urgent trip to the Anasazi ruins of Mesa Verde to resolve the riddle of one of these deaths, Kincaid reluctantly agrees. Soon, he and a van full of misfits are on the way to the cliff dwellings of the "ancestral enemies," where flesh-and-blood enemies await them among the ruins.

This sets the stage for *Places the Dead Call Home*.

Josh Kincaid is happy with life in Phoenix, where he manages a bar and sells a few drugs on the side. His serenity is soon shattered, however, by a call from his cousin, Frankie McKnight, who claims to know why Josh's father died many years earlier far from his Detroit home in the parking lot of a gas station in Oklahoma City.

General Herman Endicott is looking for Josh, too. The highlight of his military life was winning the Silver Star for bravery in Vietnam, followed a few years later by his promotion to General. But between those events, the death of a friend and the betrayal of an old comrade have brought disgrace to a bereaved widow and her unborn child. This secret could destroy the General, and Josh Kincaid may know that secret.

General Endicott hires Tommy Three Hands, an Indian living in the Phoenix area, to kill Josh and Frankie, along with a reporter named Jeffrey Bonus and his traveling companion, Jeanette Koskos, who have also shown up with questions about the death of Bonus's father. Tommy is an ex-con who distrusts and hates whites, enjoys a reputation for violence and betrayal, and has a cruel streak when it comes to women. He also has a grudge against Josh and his cousin Frankie.

All these characters converge on Mesa Verde, where the secret of the mysterious—and perhaps violent—disappearance of the Anasazi still seems to inhabit the ruins. As Josh and Frankie seek the answer to Jimmy Kincaid's destiny in the park's mythic heritage and Bonus hopes to learn the true fate of his father, Tommy and the General are making plans of their own to ensure that the dead stay where they belong—the places they call home.

Elements of a Submission Package for Children's Books

You'll need a slightly different combination of sections to submit a children's book:

1. A title page
2. A table of contents for the submission package
3. An author bio
4. A one-page description of potential markets
5. Your completed manuscript
6. A sample illustration, if you choose to include one

As you can see, you need not include a synopsis, book proposal, or chapter-by-chapter sketch. The entire manuscript should speak for itself.

Including a Sample Illustration

Only include a sample illustration if you are capable of either illustrating your book yourself or if you already have an artist you plan to use. Please also be aware that only an 8½" × 11" black-and-white sample illustration needs to be included. In addition, know that less than half of potential children's book publishers accept outside illustrators. Most prefer to use their own. Thus, the literary agents you are submitting to may be cool on the idea as well. But don't let this deter you if you are either determined to illustrate your own book, or if you have an artist outside of the publishing industry you are determined to work with.

Preparing to Create the Submission Package

The first rule in composing a submission package is that you have to make your educated, professional readers feel that what you have to offer is worthy of their time, and at the same time aid them in understanding the potential of your project. To do this can seem an insurmountable task. In fact, no other activity causes my students more strife. Luckily, I have a solution for dealing with this dilemma.

I find that all those who come to me, after completing the exercises in Part I of this book, receive a vision or an image in their mind. This vision offers all that they need to know to understand their thrust of, and reason behind, their desires to write. Here's an example of what someone might feel and see: *The author felt himself born to write. At the age of three, when most children just scribble, the author actually tried to form words during his play with crayons and pencils. He was one of the lone students in his school district who actually loved English grammar classes, and he volunteered to be the editor of the high school newspaper while only in the eighth grade. . . .* Writers may have easily been able to understand this vision when it came to them, but communicating it under the pressure of review and judgment of literary agents as part of a submission package is another thing altogether.

In the vast majority of cases, the pressure to communicate their message was far too great. They cracked, and some were left unable to write at all. Many never made it beyond this point. Those who did oftentimes had to work through dozens of drafts to regain their well-formed literary voices, which had been buried by their overreactions to the situation.

The Letter-Writing Technique

I knew that there had to be an easier way around this dilemma, something that would enable them to retain their literary voices and complete the necessary work smoothly and efficiently. It was during one of my lectures on the topic that the inspiration came to me.

Why not have my students form the basis of their synopsis or proposal by composing a letter to a close friend, with whom they obviously would feel very comfortable? Yes, that was it! It has been a long-recognized fact that we do our finest writing when communicating with someone that we know and trust. If we simply approached a close and dear comrade with a letter describing what we wanted to do and how we were going to do it, not only would our most natural voice reveal itself, but the style would only have to be altered slightly to become the synopsis or proposal that we wanted it to be.

The technique worked so well that I have been using it ever since, saving aspiring writers dozens of useless drafts and, in the most extreme cases,

Writer's
REFLECTION

Get in a deep, relaxed state. Upon opening your eyes, begin your letter with, "Dear ___, I have a great idea for a book." Then take off. Let your passions for your idea be your guide. Empty yourself onto the paper. Act as if it has been a substantial time since you have last spoken to your friend and that he or she knows nothing about your idea. Describe how the book idea came to you. If it's fiction, describe who the characters are; if it's nonfiction, who you think will buy it and how it would best be promoted. Mention why you feel that you are the best writer to author this story. Empty your soul onto paper.

keeping the vast majority of those I work with from giving up in the face of the rigors of this step.

The Divine Writer Within below is such a letter. Remember, it is very rough and doesn't in any way showcase the author's exceptionally refined writing ability. The point of reading it is to grasp the emotion behind this unique, idea-formulating technique.

the divine writer within

Dear Tom,

I have a great idea for a book about when people learn to think reflectively. From my years in the classroom, I learned that when students think superficially and do not get involved with the task, they score poorly. A good memory will get students high scores on multiple-choice tests without the benefit of really learning or understanding much. Students learn to play the "game" of school, sometimes spending more time avoiding involvement than it would take to learn the lesson. These students, and I think they are the majority, graduate from high school with little reading and writing practice, getting by doing as little as possible. Although they may or may not go to college, they are not lifelong learners. I call these passive learners "aliterates" because although they are able to decode and encode, it is in the area of comprehension that their thinking skills are lacking.

Actually, I want you to know that this is not only my opinion; the National Assessment of Educational Progress has found plenty of evidence that agrees with my theory. In fact, the great school reform movement in the late 1980s was a direct result of these test scores, which revealed that students could read and write, but they were not very good at thinking. If you remember, there were several books concerned with education on the bestseller list. You probably remember *Cultural Literacy, Frames of Mind, Among Schoolchildren,*

High School, and *The Closing of the American Mind.* Responses to these publications indicate that there is presently a national concern for teaching and learning in American schools.

Unfortunately, I have to add that my work at the college level with student teachers and their cooperating teachers has given me reason to believe that many teachers are not "thinkers" either. Kids need role models. "Do as I say, not as I do," doesn't work well. Recently I read a book by Howard Gardner entitled, *The Unschooled Mind* (1991), which really made an impression on me. Anyway, Gardner writes, "Children read not because they are told—let alone ordered—to read, but because they see adults around them reading, enjoying their reading, and using that reading productively for their own purposes, ranging from assembling a piece of apparatus to laughing at a tall tale." I am convinced that this is true, not only when it comes to reading, but also, to thinking.

There is one more thing I want to mention that brought me to the point of thinking that I could write a book about thinking. You see, I have been thinking about thinking for some time now. The term educators use when they discuss "thinking about thinking" is metacognition, which means that a person can be aware of his own thinking processes. In other words, I'm sure you have talked to yourself or questioned your own motives for doing something. I tell my student teachers that it is one thing to recall the lesson or to describe what the kids did, but they have an added benefit if they think about the students' perspective, or what they could have done differently, or if time could have been spent more wisely. I heard a teacher say once, "Boy, the whole class did poorly on that test. Those kids must not have studied"—the idea that it may have been a "poor" test never entered the teacher's mind.

Secondly, along the same line, I have done a great deal of research on writing. I wrote my dissertation on writing, I go to conventions on writing, I attend seminars on writing, and occasionally, I conduct writing workshops for English teachers. My doctoral degree is in language communications, and I am well aware of the theoretical and practical approaches to teaching and learning reading and writing. Furthermore, everything that I have been reading lately connects writing to thinking.

The last thing I need to bring up is what teachers refer to as Bloom's Taxonomy of Educational Objectives, which describes six levels of cognition. The levels are 1) knowledge—recall information, 2) comprehension—summarize or paraphrase, 3) application—relate to a prior experience, 4) analysis—classify, categorize, compare parts, 5) synthesis—put together in a new way, and 6) evaluation—make informed judgments and support opinion. Originally, the taxonomy was thought of as a hierarchy, meaning that you had to teach at level one before going to level two, but today it is used as a simple way to look at how thinking skills are related to teaching and learning. However, there is plenty of research to indicate that what we teach in schools is mainly lower-level thinking, tasks that require recall and paraphrase at the knowledge and comprehension levels. Generally, we think of application, analysis, synthesis, and evaluation as higher-order thinking skills. Perhaps this is another reason that students score poorly on higher-level thinking skills.

The good news is, we do know how to teach and learn these skills. It seems to me that most of us reach a point in time when we realize that it is important to think clearly, or at least we see a need for being a better thinker. How many times have you said, "I just didn't think"? The drunk driver has said it. The inexperienced hunter has said it. Young mothers have said it. Habits of thinking can be improved quite easily. For example, if your child complains about an assignment at school, ask him what the teacher could have done to make it a better learning experience, or, if your child wants to write a letter to the editor of a newspaper because bicycles aren't allowed on sidewalks, take a moment to have him think about other points of view—the elderly who may not see well, parents of small children, or homeowners liable for injuries on their property.

To tell you the truth, Tom, I read a book once and I quit smoking. I read a book and I got organized. I read a book and I made a quilt. Last week there was an article in the *Wall Street Journal* about entrepreneurs who began with a "How To" book. Why not a book about thinking?

Boni

Deciding on a Literary Agent

If you are fortunate enough to have more than one literary agency offer you representation, which is what this entire system has been designed to do, think long and hard about which representative you choose.

When you've narrowed it down to two or three possible agents, call the agencies who have offered you contracts and ask them the following questions, along with any other queries you may have come up with on your own.

1. **How many publishers will you initially be submitting my work to?**
    Getting the best deal from a traditional publisher means giving your book its best chance to succeed. The best way to guarantee that you are getting the best deal is to create a competition for it. To be able to do that, normally referred to by agents as an "auction," your representative needs to initially approach a minimum of a dozen publishers.

CHECK OUT THIS SITE

Subscribe to *www.publishermarketplace.com* for at least one month and then go onto the agents' sites and check out even further the ones who are interested in you. Publishersmarketplace.com lists the majority of sales for agents for the past few years. See which publishers the agents who you are interested in are selling to and for how much are they selling the books they represent. Also check out the number of books they have sold within the last six months, and what types of books were sold.

2. **How soon will my material be in the hands of publishers?** With this question, you are gauging the degree of interest a perspective literary agent has in you and your material. If, after having received the necessary material from you to approach publishers, it takes them longer than ten days to get it into the right hands, they are either not that interested or incompetent.

3. **How long do you anticipate that it will take to land me an acceptable offer from a publisher?** Six weeks for a nonfiction proposal package is good. Four to six months for a first novel is acceptable.

4. **What type of dollar amount do they expect a publisher to be willing to risk on you and your book through an advance?** (You should definitely expect to receive an advance from a traditional publisher. The agent has 15 percent riding on your advance, so he/she will demand an advance too.) First of all, let me clarify that no agent, because of the subjectivity of the market, will be comfortable answering this question. Yet, it is still one you have to ask, for you need to know if what they will be shooting for is in line with what the market bears. How do you know if that is that case? By this point, you should have already checked out *www.publishersmarketplace.com* and tracked the amount of money paid for books that are similar to yours. Keep in mind that the upfront money you will be referring to is an advance, which translates to "risk money applied against royalties earned."

After you have asked all your questions and concluded your interviews, decide whom you will be signing with. After you've made your decision and have properly informed your choice, contact your other final candidates, explaining which agency you went with and why. Make sure that you don't burn any bridges with the finalists you didn't choose. You want that door open to reapproach them in the future if, for some reason, your relationship with the agent you did choose doesn't work out.

Contracts with Agents

The next step is to sign a contract with your chosen agent. Because of the significant role your literary agent will play in your eventual success, the contract you will sign with him or her is the most important of your young writing career. There are only three types of agent-author agreements. Here they are, listed from the worst to the best.

A Time-Related Agreement

A time-related agreement basically states that any and all works that you compose will be the sole responsibility of a specific literary agent to market over a certain period of time, usually two years. Though this sort of agreement greatly benefits a literary agent, it is the worst possible contractual relationship an author can enter into. The reason is simple: you will be giving away all the representative rights of all your works for a significant period of time to an agency that you cannot guarantee is the best to handle your work. And if you have made a mistake in your decision to go with a certain agency, who pays most for the mistake? You do, via lost opportunities, in addition to having to potentially buy your way out of such an agreement if you discover that the agent you chose is not the right one for you.

A Project-Related Agreement

Project-related agreements carry a significant amount of liability on your end as well, but not nearly as much as its time-related counterpart. A project-related agreement states that you are allowing a literary agency to solely handle the representative rights to a specific project or projects. But what happens if the literary agent you signed on with under this sort of design doesn't turn out to be the right one for you? Again, you may have to buy your way out of your agreement to take your project to another representative.

There is a way to make this sort of agreement more livable. Simply make sure it is stated in your contract that if your book project is not sold within a certain period of time (usually one year is very fair), for an acceptable amount, then you can choose to cancel your agreement with the literary agent at no cost. This caveat will allow you to go somewhere else without having to pay your former literary agent for any job he or she was unable to do.

Open-Ended Agreements

An open-ended contract is the best agreement that you can hope for, because it allows you to cancel your commitment with a literary agent at any time with no penalty to you. Varieties of this sort of agreement range from verbal agreements to typical written agreements.

Other Contractual Considerations

Besides the main structure of your contract, investigate the following facets and be sure your contract is fair and thorough.

EXPENSES

If a literary agent charges you expenses outside of mailing costs, typing costs (if needed), and copying costs (if needed), he is probably getting some sort of kickback from the expenditures. Legitimate literary agents derive their incomes only from the commissions via sales of books. If literary agents have to charge for padded expenses, they're probably not doing their job. If that's the case, what does that tell you? They're not very good salespeople, which is their primary function to you, and, thus, probably not the right literary agents for you or anyone else.

HIDDEN COSTS

If literary agents try to rope you into a contract that obligates you to pay for editing fees, rewriting fees, consultation fees, or anything like these, they're not worth your time. Again, like those who over-emphasize expenses, and probably severely pad them, they're probably not bringing in enough commission to support themselves and their business, so they turn to less honest means to acquire their income. Literary agents who hit you with hidden costs are not only not worth your time, but could prove to be extremely dangerous to your career. Avoid these people.

the divine writer
within

As strongly as I stress that each of my students follow exactly the steps I am laying out for you in this book, some of them nonetheless miss or just outwardly avoid doing one of the tasks I have laid out. Such was the case for a student of mine from the West Coast, who chose not to thoroughly interview each of the agents interested in her book before signing a contract with one. The end result?

She lost between $220,000 and $330,000 as the result of some lazy miscues that were made by her agent. She chose an agent based entirely on her personality rather than on her contacts in the publishing industry. Thus, she sold her project to a publisher who paid far less for it than another would have. Unfortunately, this agent's lack of contacts at those larger publishers cost this author money.

The lesson: Make sure to follow each one of the steps to choose just the right literary agent for your book. If you do, you'll avoid lost time and money and give your book its best chance at success.

Commonly Asked Questions about Submitting Your Writing

Here are questions I answer frequently about the proposal process.

How long do I have to send my submission package after getting a positive response from an agent?

It is of the utmost importance that your submission package be a good representation of both you and your idea. How long it will take to get it there is up to you. Simply inform your interested sources when you feel that you will be able to get your package to them. Unless yours is a very timely piece, and the chances are small that it will be, they are usually more than happy to wait. At the same time, it shows a significant amount of efficiency on your end if you politely keep them abreast of your progress on a monthly basis. It also doesn't allow them to lose you among the many writers who contact them on a daily, weekly, and monthly basis.

Should I have my material bound before submitting it?

Securing your pages in a plastic spiral binding may seem to add an aura of professionalism to any submission. But it is not a necessity, nor is it expected by those who will receive your submission. In fact, some literary agents and editors detest spiral bindings because they make photocopying your work much harder (which they'll need to do to distribute work to their colleagues).

How long should a synopsis or proposal be?

Neither has any presupposed length. Each should simply and thoroughly introduce your idea, telling all that needs to be told, to fully enlighten your sources to the depth, scope, and potential of your project.

How much do I have to pay a literary agent?

If a literary agent charges you any more than a commission of between 10 and 15 percent, plus expecting you to reimburse them for reasonable out-of-pocket expenses (long distance costs, mailing expenses, and any typing or copying costs, if necessary), there's a good chance that you are dealing with a less-than-worthy source. Stay clear of such people. Their inability to properly market books has probably led them to seek an income in less than honest ways.

What should I do when an agency asks to review my material on an exclusive basis?

Do not deceive an agency into thinking you are giving them an exclusive shot at your work when you're not. Just arrange your submission strategy to accommodate their request. Or even better, you can guarantee an agency asking for an exclusive look that you will not select any other agency for representation before hearing back from them, as long as they reply in a timely fashion of no more than three weeks after receipt.

Above all, it's important to be honest at all times.

Conclusion

Now that you've landed the representative of your dreams, let's explore how to maintain a great working relationship with him or her.

chapter twelve

Waiting for Your Book to Find a Publisher

YES, IT'S EXCITING to select a literary agent and begin shopping your book around to publishers. But your work doesn't stop here. There are still three basic activities you are responsible for while you wait for your book to find a suitable publisher.

Activity #1: Dispel Your Doubt

This phase of the publishing process brings great excitement and exhilaration. Yet these feelings, if not properly channeled, could lead to rampant confusion, doubt, and frustration. The confusion and doubt often show up in response to your great success and fortune. Yes, there is a downside to those things! In many cases, writers have a difficult time believing what is happening to them—they are shocked that what they wanted for so long has appeared at all, let alone so fast. As a result, doubts start to dominate their minds.

No matter how refined you try to act in these circumstances, there's an excellent chance that you may become unwound because of the life-altering impact of this arrangement and situation. If you let your emotions get the best of you, you could ruin and then dissolve the valuable relationship that you waited so long for and worked so hard to acquire. For example, you could contact your agent *waaaaayyy* too much with probing questions and a doubting attitude, until he or she just wants to get you out of his or her life. That is *not* the working relationship you want to have.

To prevent yourself from experiencing this form of self-sabotage, set up some sort of communication routine with your agent where he or she checks in with you via phone or e-mail every three to four weeks, and then stick to it. Don't let your fears, worries, doubts, and concerns get the better of you. Using this technique, you will receive the timely updates you deserve, but you'll still be giving your agent the time, space, trust, and freedom that he or she needs to do the job.

> **Pearl of *Wisdom***
>
> In this industry, the squeaky wheel doesn't get greased, it gets replaced, *especially* if it is a brand-new wheel.

I know it's tough to relax and back off, but using this communication arrangement will pay off. Your agent will appreciate your professionalism and will reward you by devoting more of his or her energy to the sale of your work (rather than fielding calls from you demanding an update). Your sane and professional approach will also make you stand out favorably from the other clients that he or she represents. As a result, you will get better service and he or she will be able to boast about you to the potential purchasers of your work as a model client—and believe me, that means a *lot* in today's high-stress, crazy, emotional publishing world.

Sedona Secret
RESPECT AND TRUST

It's important to remember two words during this time period: respect and trust. Treat your agent with them and you will likely receive them in return. *Respect* his or her experience and knowledge, and *trust* that he or she will sell your work to a suitable publisher.

Activity #2: Study Up on Author Contracts

Use the time while your work is being shopped around to study the following material on publishing agreements. Doing so will not only prepare you to make the proper decisions when your contract comes through, but you will be sending out good vibes from yourself to all associated with the project, through your cheerful, optimistic, always upbeat disposition, as well. Since I could not do such a vast topic justice in this book, I'll refer you to *How to Understand a Book Contract* and *A Writer's Guide to Book Publishing* by Richard Balkin instead. They offer a thorough review of author book contracts.

Activity #3: Begin Your Second Book

Believe it or not, writing again is probably the most important step that you can take to benefit yourself, your agent, and the eventual elevation of your goals as a writer. I know that your LCB is probably telling you that doing so is crazy. "I mean, shouldn't I wait until the first one is sold before I go wasting time on working on another one?"

No. Go ahead and start work on that next project now. You'll have to just take my advice here. But, toss the following rock-solid reasons at your old LCB to see if they will better ease its concerns:

1. Working on a second project might help distract you so you're able to give your agent the time, space, and freedom he or she needs to best complete the sale of your work.
2. Your second book will most likely be better than your first. As a result, it may have a better chance of selling. In fact, in my estimation, my students' second works are written about three times better than their first works. Why? You have expended so much time and energy learning to write during your first book that there is little time left to address the actual inspiration as it comes through you. That reverses with your second

171

book—your inspiration will lead the way. And more inspiration will make your work a more powerful read.

3. You're a writer, and writers write. You're not a professional telephone watcher who just sits around waiting for your agents to call (even though you may be hard-pressed to find an agent who would agree with me on that point).

4. You're probably already in good writing "shape," and you might as well take advantage of it.

5. Having a second or third or whatever number project ready to go to market provides you with that many more opportunities to succeed. Remember the primary point in this section, though: *Make yourself different. Make yourself special. Conduct yourself professionally, and you'll be amazed at the results.*

Commonly Asked Questions about Getting Your Book Sold

How long will it take for my book to be sold?

It depends on several factors (the aggressiveness and knowledge of your literary agent, the quality of your material, the mindset of the publishing industry at the time of your submission), most of which are out of your control.

The best way to answer this question for yourself is to ask your literary agent's opinion on how long it will take your material to be sold. Do this before you sign a contract with him or her, and it will help you gauge how aggressive they plan to be.

Should I use a pen name?

The name you choose to put on the cover of your work is totally up to you. The only time it is really necessary to use a pen name is when you deliberately want to hide your affiliation with a project. One example of that situation is if you're writing a similar book or two that will also be available soon, such as a romance author releasing two new works at the same time.

Can I really make a living doing this?

Definitely! In fact, with the ever-expanding media markets, there has never been a better time than today to be a writer. Also, writing is one of those rare professions that doesn't place any weight on your age, gender, sexual preference, education, color, or socioeconomic background. If you can write, want to write, and are willing to endure the emotional upheavals you may put yourself through with the submission of your work, you have what it takes to make it in this business.

How much money will it take for me to become an author?

Money isn't much of a factor here if you're not self-publishing. Sure, you should have a computer, and it's a good idea if you take a writing class or two. And there are costs for mailing and paper and such. But outside of that, writers pay for their successes with the sweat of their souls. The monetary investment is small, but the emotional output is great.

the divine writer within

Over the last quarter of a century, I have been both privy to and blessed to see the lives, careers, and literary destinies of authors of all ages and educational levels and from all walks of lives meet with great, and sometimes instant, success through the use of my method.

Very rarely does a week go by that I do not receive some great news from at least one of my students whose book was just recently released or

Writer's
REFLECTION

Grab a few minutes and write down the story of your literary success, step-by-step (after you have sold, published, or completed your book), and send it to me at *TomBird@ TomBird.com.* Not only would I love to see it, but, with your permission, I would also like to share it with others to better encourage them to accomplish their literary dreams. Thank you in advance for doing so. You're unselfishly extending yourself to others who may not be able to accomplish what they will without you, your insight, your heart, and your encouragement.

published. Here are just a few examples of what they have had to say over the years.

Dear Tom,

I wish to thank you for all you have done to make a difference in the thousands of individual lives you have reached, including mine. Your writing workshop at the University of Tennessee and your excellent books have made a huge impact on my writing over the past six years. As the result of your help I have completed four books and am enclosing you a copy of my latest publication, *Per Usual, James Roy.*

Best regards,
David Puckett

Hello Tom,

It has been awhile and you may not remember me, but I took your class at Emory in Atlanta many moons ago—I want to say March 2000. I have written all my life, but your class, your program, your way of "bringing out the book inside you" changed my life. . . . I now have a book contract with Skyhorse Publishing out of New York! The book is called *Freddie and Me: Life Lessons from the Legendary Augusta National Caddy Master.* It is scheduled for release March 1, 2009, to coincide with the Masters tournament. Currently it is listed on Amazon as well as a few other sites for presell! Pretty wild.

I have also written a 1,200-page novel that my agent is currently shopping around (*Greyhound Jesus and the Perpetual Care Fund*), and also have another proposal out on the market. None of this happens without you.

The reason for my e-mail is a simple one. I want to say thank you. Thank you for giving me hope, for opening the door to life-changing events. . . . I know I'm just getting started, and who knows how the book will sell, but I am dreaming big. Why dream at all if you don't dream big? . . .

So thank you again, Tom. Thank you for waking me up to the writer I was born to be.

All the best,
Tripp Bowden

"I've been a writer all of my life really, but it wasn't until I met Tom Bird, and took his Writer's Success Series at Scottsdale Community College, that I released my author within. Through Tom's inspiration and step-by-step plan, I was able to visualize my book—from its cover to a basic content—and begin the process of writing. Taking Tom's advice, I asked my family for the gift of time over the holiday. Two weeks of uninterrupted time to dedicate to my book! It was truly a spiritual experience as some days I would look back and read what flowed from my pen, and wonder, "who wrote that?" I've been blessed by Tom's enthusiasm and his sharing of insights into the world of successful writers. I've now published *The Dance of Defiance: A Mother and Son Journey with Oppositional Defiant Disorder* to positive reviews. More importantly, I've been told that my book has touched hearts and changed lives. I believe Tom would agree, that's what it's all about.

—Nancy A. Hagener, author of *Dance of Defiance:*
A Mother and Son Journey with Oppositional Defiant Disorder
(Shamrock Books)

Tom,

Please accept this with my gratitude. I'd not have finished *Arcturus* were it not for your course.

—Mike Mollenhour, author of *Arcturus* (Talavera Media)

Conclusion

It can be tough to wait for that phone call announcing that a publisher has offered you a contract, but you must be patient. After all, you've waited this long in your life for this opportunity—don't let your anxiety and excitement overtake your common sense.

conclusion

The Most Important Law in Regard to Getting Published

LISTEN. THAT'S RIGHT, listen. If you listen, you will learn. If you learn, you will understand; if you understand, you will grow; and if you grow, you will succeed. But it all begins with *listening*.

The people you will be listening to are your prospective literary agents, editors, and publishers. These people might offer you suggestions. But they will only do so if they see potential in you and your work, and their comments will help you reach that potential. That doesn't mean you should take their advice verbatim, but you would be missing a huge opportunity to grow and succeed faster if you didn't listen. Whatever you do with their suggestions is up to you. But listen: this industry will teach you everything that you need to learn if you do.

Because each of us has been hurt at one time or another during our lives in response to creatively expressing ourselves. The greater the amount of time between when that initial blow took place and now, the greater the defensiveness on our end. It's that defensiveness that could keep you from hearing what could benefit you the most. Don't allow that to happen to you. Shrug off the past, close your mouth, open your ears, and listen. If you are asked to take into consideration some suggestions to improve your work, and you agree with them, then do it. That doesn't mean that you have to adhere to everything. But listen. You may just learn something that will greatly contribute to the speed and breadth of your eventual success.

You'll never be the same after embarking on your writing career. You'll just keep getting better and better at publishing and happier and happier as you go.

Remember to listen first to your Divine Writer Within and then listen to all of the messengers, whether they come in the forms of TAs or PAs. They will lead you where your soul is calling you to go, proving to you that you were born to be published.

I promise.

—Tom Bird

appendix a

Checklist of
Responsibilities for
Self-Publication

AS WE DISCUSSED in Chapter 8, if you decide to self-publish, you'll need to tackle a number of tasks on your own. Here is a slightly modified checklist as designed by one of my students—Shirley Hildreth of Muse Imagery in Las Vegas, Nevada—that outlines what you'll need to do and when. Shirley has become so successful at organizing this system that she has now begun working with new authors in leading them through this process. At the conclusion of Shirley's checklist, I have included some of her sample announcements and review response forms.

Step One: Your Business Foundation

❏ Form a corporation

❏ Acquire an Employer Identification Number

❏ Acquire a sales tax/state business license

❏ Acquire city business license

NOTES

_____

_____

_____

_____

_____

_____

_____

_____

_____

_____

_____

_____

_____

_____

Step Two: Your Book

- ❑ Write book
- ❑ Choose size
- ❑ Decide on a price
- ❑ Choose a cover designer
- ❑ Choose text formatter for layout and design
- ❑ Choose potential copyeditor
- ❑ Choose potential style editor
- ❑ Compile illustrations, gather photographs
- ❑ Write extraneous information:
    - ❑ Author's bio
    - ❑ Acknowledgments
    - ❑ Dedication
    - ❑ Contact page
    - ❑ Order page
    - ❑ Jacket copy
- ❑ Acquire accolades/endorsements
- ❑ Get permission slips (to use endorsements) signed

NOTES

_____

_____

_____

_____

_____

_____

_____

Step Three: Protecting Your Product

❑ Consider acquiring a trademark

❑ Acquire trademark verification from an attorney

❑ Acquire a copyright from the Library of Congress; text: $30

❑ Acquire a copyright from the Library of Congress; cover: $30

❑ Acquire a copyright from the Library of Congress; published book: Form TX within three months of printing 2 copies of book plus $35.00

❑ Acquire Library of Congress preassigned control number (PCN— which is printed in the book and helps cataloging and other book processing activities); *www.loc.gov*

❑ Acquire Library of Congress Cataloging in Publication Division (CIP); send book. (You are only eligible to participate in the CIP program after you have published three books.)

❑ Acquire Bowker International Standard Business Number (ISBN): *www.bowkerlink.com*

❑ Acquire Bowker Registration: *www.bowkerlink.com*

NOTES

_____

_____

_____

_____

_____

_____

_____

_____

_____

_____

_____

Step Four: Promotion

- ❏ Construct a media/news kit
- ❏ Collect testimonials
- ❏ Write suggested interview questions (this makes it easier on the media person)
- ❏ Write press release
- ❏ Choose excerpt from your book
- ❏ Construct a sample flyer
- ❏ Write a news/press release
- ❏ Design promotional bookmarks as handout
- ❏ Design a business card
- ❏ Design stationery
- ❏ Design a website
- ❏ Join the Publishers Marketing Association: *www.pma-online.org*
- ❏ Join the American Association of Publishers
- ❏ Join the American Booksellers Association: *www.bookweb.org*
  ABA BookBuyer's Handbook: *www.bookweb.com*
- ❏ List with the Contemporary Authors: *www.galegroup.com*
- ❏ List in International Directory of Little Mag & Small Press: *www.dustbooks.com*
- ❏ List in the Literary Marketplace: *www.literarymarketplace.com*
- ❏ List in the Publishers Directory: *www.galegroup.com*
- ❏ List in the Small Press Record of Books In Print (also International Dir.): *www.dustbooks.com*
- ❏ List in Bowker Books In Print: *www.bowkers.com*
- ❏ Enhance Listing on Amazon.com: *www.amazon.com*
- ❏ Enhance Listing on Barnes & Noble: *www.barnesandnoble.com*
- ❏ Enhance Listing on Books a Million: *www.booksamillion.com*
- ❏ List on *www.seekbooks.com*
- ❏ List on *www.elgrande.com*

NOTES

Step Five: Submit for Reviews

❑ Baker & Taylor: *www.btol.com*

❑ Booklist (American Library Association): *www.ala.org/booklist*

❑ *Chicago Tribune* Books: *www.chicagotribune.com/leisure/books*

❑ *Forward Magazine*: *www.forwardmagazine.com*

❑ H. W. Wilson Co.: *www.hwwilson.com*

❑ Independent Publisher: *www.bookpublishing.com*

❑ Ingram Book Group: *www.ingrambookgroup.com*

❑ Kirkus Reviews: *www.kirkusreviews.com*

❑ Library Journal: *www.libraryjournal.com*

❑ *Los Angeles Times* Book Review: *www.latimes.com*

❑ Midwest Book Review: *www.execpc.com/~mbr/bookwatch*

❑ *Newsday*: *www.newsday.com*

❑ *New York Review of Books: www.nybooks.com*

❑ *New York Times* (send out first): *www.nytimes.com/books*

❑ *Publishers Weekly: www.publishersweekly.com*

❑ Rainbo Electronic Reviews: *www.rainboreviews.com*

❑ *Reader's Digest* Select Editions: *www.readersdigest.com*

❑ Ruminator Review: *www.ruminator.com*

❑ *San Francisco Chronicle*: *www.sfgate.com/eguide/books*

❑ Small Press Review: *www.dustbooks.com*

❑ *USA Today: www.usatoday.com*

❑ *Voice* Literary Supplement: *www.villagevoice.com*

❑ *Washington Post* (send out first): *www.washingtonpost.com*

NOTES

_____

_____

_____

_____

Step Six: Submit to Book Clubs

❑ *www.literarymarketplace.com*

❑ Book-of-the-Month Club: *www.bookspan.com*

❑ Doubleday Select: *www.booksonline.com*

❑ Literary Guild: *www.literaryguild.com*

❑ Writer's Digest Book Club: *www.writersdigest.com*

NOTES

_____

_____

_____

_____

_____

_____

_____

_____

_____

_____

_____

_____

_____

Step Seven: Other

❑ Contact radio/TV talk shows

❑ Design author promotion tour

❑ Schedule autograph parties

❑ Schedule speaking engagements

❑ Schedule book fairs

❑ Schedule Book Expo America (annually in May/June): *www.bookexpo.com*

❑ Consider Frankfurt Book Fair (October in Germany): *www.frankfurt-book-fair.com*

NOTES

_____

_____

_____

_____

_____

_____

_____

_____

_____

_____

_____

_____

Prepublication Review Mailing

These documents should be sent out four to five months prior to publish date:

❏ Cover letter

❏ Bound galley with book review slip as cover (Book Review Slip sample shown on page 189)

❏ News release

❏ Author bio including a section listing "Future Books by the Author"

❏ Fax response transmittal sheet (sample shown on page 190)

❏ SASE addressed to the publisher (the cover letter requested a clipping/tear sheet of the review)

NOTES

_____

_____

_____

_____

_____

_____

_____

_____

_____

_____

_____

_____

_____

Postpublication Review Mailing

❑ Cover letter

❑ Published book

❑ Book review slip included as an informational 8½" x 11" sheet

❑ 4" x 6" (or larger) photo of book cover

❑ Flyer/brochure

❑ Testimonials

❑ News release

❑ Author bio

❑ Expanded informational sheet explaining the question, What makes this book unique?

❑ Expanded informational sheet explaining, Who is the audience for this book?

❑ Fax response transmittal sheet (shown on page 190)

❑ SASE addressed to the publisher (the cover letter requested a clipping/tear sheet of the review)

I used a professional border around all of the documents included in this mailing.

NOTES

_____

_____

_____

_____

_____

_____

_____

_____

_____

_____

Sample Book Review Slip: Prepublication

Spiritually Enlightening Thoughts™:
Teaching Children How to Connect with God
Shirley Hildreth

Category: Religion (adult)/Family and (**BISG Major subjects**) Relationships/Self-Help
Edition: First Edition
Specifications: Soft cover; 7" x 9"; 128 pages; illustrated
Season: Winter, 2003
Price: $19.95
ISBN No.: 0-9740500-0-8
LOC Control No.: 2003094617
Intended Audience: Parents, clergy and teachers of children in a religious setting, extended family members, psychologists, and caregivers of children.
Promotional Plans: Author tour, space advertising, direct mail, writer's conferences
Distribution: Ingram Book Group
Trademarks: SETS: Spiritually Enlightening Thoughts and Muse Imagery are trademarks of Muse Imagery LLC, a Nevada Limited Liability Co.
Description: SETS: *Teaching Children to Connect with God* is a book about a teaching method called Spiritually Enlightening Thoughts (SETS)™ and builds on the premise that thoughts precede actions and that God-based thoughts bring about God-based actions. It shares anecdotes to help readers understand their role in teaching children this most valuable lesson, and provides teaching modules to enable them to do so.

Readers are invited to slow down and change focus to look for a spiritual meaning and purpose to life then share what they have learned with a child. It speaks of the great potential of each child, and the child that lives within each of us, no matter what our circumstances, and how we, as adults, must nurture this potential so that it will blossom and flourish. The book is nondenominational.

Sample Facsimile Transmittal Sheet

MUSE IMAGERY
9811 W. Charleston Blvd. Suite 2390 • Las Vegas, NV 89117

Muse Imagery Facsimile Transmittal Sheet

To: Jane Smith, Reviewer
From: Marketing Director, MUSE IMAGERY
Fax Number: 702-123-4567
Phone Number: 702-123-4567
E-Mail: marketing@museimagery.com
Total number of pages: 1
Re: BOOK REVIEW ACKNOWLEDGMENT

We have received the book review galley(s) for: *SETS™ Teaching Children How to Connect with God.*

❑ We expect to review this book on _____.

❑ We expect to review this book, however the exact date is uncertain at this time.

❑ Please send photograph of book to:
E-mail address _____

❑ Please send photograph of author to:
E-mail address _____

❑ We are sorry, we did not find your book suitable for review at this time.

Additional Comments:

_____

_____

_____

---

appendix b

Sample Query Letters

Fiction Sample

Basketball and Past Lives
Written by award-winning filmmaker
Ken Feinberg

Rudy meets *What Dreams May Come* in this novel by award-winning filmmaker, published playwright, and LA Drama Critics Circle Award nominated playwright Ken Feinberg. Screenplay and feature film to follow.

As a senior at the University of Alabama, Ace makes a surprise impression on basketball Coach Hill in a charity basketball game. In the game, Ace covers Alabama star and NCAA tournament MVP Ice. When Coach Hill departs to coach in the NBA, he invites Ace to camp for a tryout along with #1 draft pick Ice. Not only does Ace make the team, but he also becomes the catalyst that catapults himself, Ice, and the lowly Atlanta Hawks toward their first championship run.

During the championship series, Coach Fitzsimmons, of the Timberwolves, will do anything to win a championship ring after being denied for so long. He sends his two ruffians in the game to explicitly knock Ace out of it. They knock Ace too hard, sending him out of the game and into a coma.

While Ace lies unconscious in the hospital, he experiences his last two lives: One as Simon, a Jewish museum curator in Berlin, Germany, just before the war, and the other as Kahiga, an American Indian shaman in training. As the shaman, Kahiga travels forward in time and witnesses his demise in Germany. Then, he visits Ace (himself) in the hospital in a coma.

Kahiga explains to Ace about the mistakes he keeps repeating each lifetime, and how his decision now will affect his past lives as well as his future lives. Ace has the decision to opt out now and start over, or make some major changes in his life.

-continued-

Fiction Sample (continued)

Ace sees how Ice has been his best friend in many lives; Coach Hill, his mentor; and Coach Fitzsimmons and his two goons recurring enemies.

Basketball and Past Lives is a great story that combines action/ sports with metaphysical insight and drama. For young adult readers as well as adult readers.

Thank you for your consideration. I look forward to hearing from you.

Sincerely,
Ken Feinberg
123 Any Street
Your Town, USA

Update: Ken received almost two dozen positive replies to his query letter.

Fiction Sample

MAUREEN SIOBHAN MOORE, ESQ.
123 Any Street, EL PRADO, NM 87529
(123) 123-1234
anyauthor@aol.com

The Mistresses Club

The Mistresses Club combines strong, funny, outspoken, believable characters like those in Jennifer Crusie's *Welcome to Temptation*, with an underlying message of hope like Marian Keyes's *Rachel's Holiday* and *Lucy Sullivan Is Getting Married*. But there are also shades of Armistead Maupin's *Tales of the City* in this novel about nine people—eight women and one gay man—all of whom are involved with married men in small-town Jamaica, Indiana.

Bright, witty, red-headed realtor Sally Van Neal; dumpy, straight-laced church secretary Marci Ferguson; and glamorous yet vulnerable African-American artist Desiree Thomas are the three main characters. When Sally starts a support group for mistresses, based loosely on the principles of AA, she meets Marci, who is in love with a member of her church choir, and Desiree, whose lover delights in keeping her on an emotional roller coaster.

They are joined by paralegal JoAnn Renart, whose steel-trap mind is concealed by shaggy hair and Coke-bottle glasses; twenty-two-year-old Tiffani Calder, who appears to be a stereotypical dumb blonde; and Elise Jensen, a forty-something English teacher. Gay interior designer Jesse Squires and Gina Smithson Delacourt, the richest woman in town, round out the original group. Later, after much denial, hairdresser Lisa Shepherd joins them. Their lives interweave in chance encounters at Sunday brunches, hair appointments, and a bar mitzvah, as well as in their weekly meetings.

-continued-

Fiction Sample (continued)

As the mistresses come to know each other better, deep, supportive friendships develop, sometimes between the most unlikely partners. Jesse and almost-homophobic Marci become close when she helps him in his relationship with Gina's husband. Sally, who hated Elise in high school, is a rock of support when Elise's lover kills himself. Tiffani turns to Marci, who is shocked to the core at Tiffani's family history of murder and prostitution, but is able to help her see that she is not condemned to repeat the past. When Desiree's boyfriend breaks up with her publicly, Elise is there to pick up the pieces, and Desiree eventually finds enough strength to reject him and go to Greece to paint. With help from Lisa, JoAnn gets the courage to apply to law school and leave Jamaica—and then her lover's wife tells him she wants a divorce. Marci's lover breaks up with her, and she finds a new job, a deeper faith, and a new love interest. Gina masterminds a plot to save Roger and Jesse's relationship even as she questions her motives in continuing to see her own lover. After much soul-searching and help from Lisa, Sally stays with her boyfriend, with a bittersweet knowing that their relationship is doomed. As the novel ends, some of the characters are in love relationships, some are alone, but all have grown and changed as a result of being members of *The Mistresses Club*. Their desires and motivations are as old as the Bible and as current as *Desperate Housewives*.

Update: Maureen received many positive replies to her query and is presently being represented by agent Ken Atchity.

Nonfiction Sample

Michelle DeAngelis
123 Any Street, Santa Monica, CA 90405
anyauthor@aol.com
123-345-6789
www.authorname.com

Dear [Literary Agent]:

In the tradition of groundbreaking books such as *Who Moved My Cheese?*, *Don't Sweat the Small Stuff*, and *You: The Owner's Manual*, *Get a Life That Doesn't Suck* compels the reader to get out of the rut he is in and make better choices. As the title suggests, *Get a Life That Doesn't Suck* is written to appeal to the reader who wants Deepak Chopra in a David Sedaris state of mind. It is wisdom served up as street-smart joy: an irreverent take on how to live life and love the ride. *Get a Life* is written by consultant, speaker, and coach, Michelle DeAngelis, who has been bringing a healthy dose of reality and life-affirming change to corporate America for nearly twenty years.

In Get a Life That Doesn't Suck, Michelle meets people in their misery and provides the antidote to common problems that make life seem like a succession of bad days: frustration, anger, hopelessness, feeling stuck, without energy, "checked out," paralyzed by indecision. Each of these obstacles to a joyful life is tackled with humor and real-life stories, as well as step-by-step instructions that guide the reader through the mechanics of choosing on purpose, and then owning the consequences of those choices.

Get a Life That Doesn't Suck appeals to the same audiences that loved books such as *The Joy Diet*, *How We Choose to Be Happy*, and the *Chicken Soup for the Soul* series, which prove the demand for practical and engaging books about personal power, inspiration, and human potential.

-continued-

Nonfiction Sample (continued)

The primary buyer for *Get a Life That Doesn't Suck* will be the self-improvement junkie who is continuously looking for the new and better way. The secondary buyer will be those who know people whose lives suck, and will also include career counselors, corporate human resource departments, and other professionals touting personal accountability.

Get a Life That Doesn't Suck makes it "okay" to be in a joyless existence—but not for long. It reminds us, in a playful and engaging way, how ill-equipped we are to deal with the challenges in life. Few of us are taught how to effectively work our way through problems and difficulties. Most people are taught to rail, complain, and feel victimized that things never go their way. *Get a Life That Doesn't Suck* reminds the reader what so many have forgotten or overlooked: We always have a choice. But choosing takes guts, and most people don't bother to summon the courage when it's easier to blame someone else. The book consists of three basic sections:

❑ **You Are Here.** Where IS that exactly? This part includes tools to determine the reader's starting point, such as the Joy Quotient Quiz, which gives the reader his "JQ" and measures the internal gap between his beliefs and his actions. The reader is given a chance to pick himself out of a line-up of dismal circumstances, ranging from bored, lonely, and without purpose, to mad, hung over, and racked with guilt. If it sucks, *Get a Life That Doesn't Suck* can help.

❑ **The Aha!s.** These are the basic principles to live by—the keys to the *Get a Life* kingdom—explained through irresistible stories about real people learning lessons and having fun, and they are pivotal in getting the audience from where they are now to where they want to be. These are not vague clichés, nor platitudes. The Aha!s outline the specific steps to choosing the life you want in everyday moments of truth.

-continued-

Nonfiction Sample (continued)

❏ **The Other Side.** You might even miss complaining. Once you are able to embody the Aha!s and narrow your joy gaps, here's what's on the other side: waking up happy and refreshed, having enough energy throughout the day, being able to say 'no' when you need to, losing those 15 pounds, getting that promotion, even dealing with the jackass at the dry cleaners. You choose. Next thing you know, you have a Life.

For those who are sick and tired of being sick and tired, *Get a Life That Doesn't Suck* offers a better way to go through every day. *Get a Life* encourages the reader to learn what makes him happy, what reduces his worry, what improves his outlook, what he needs to let go of, and how to do that. It makes joy accessible, and it makes the concept of enjoying life a tangible one, not an airy-fairy dream.

The journey from blame to personal power and accountability is not an easy one, but *Get a Life* makes it worth the trip.

Sincerely,
Michelle DeAngelis

Update: Michelle went on to have her very successful book published by Rodale.

Nonfiction Sample

Enclosed is a query for the book, *Forgiveness: The Ultimate Freedom*. As you can see by the enclosed letter, I have already received an endorsement from the Dalai Lama for this book.

Forgiveness: The Ultimate Freedom

In a world fraught with hatred and violence, all of us will be placed in situations challenged by issues of forgiveness. Just as Neale Donald Walsh in his books on *Conversations with God* has helped us realize that spirituality is at our fingertips, *Forgiveness: The Ultimate Freedom* will show us how we can transform our consciousness through the power of love and compassion.

The essence of this book opens people's hearts to forgive offering the all-illusive "peace of mind" we all seek. The audience for this work is unlimited, ranging from the abused to the abuser, from the young to the old, covering both genders and including millions of caregivers.

Through stories beginning with your next-door neighbor to interviews with one of our greatest spiritual leaders and with people from all walks of life who have experienced personal struggles and tragedies from the personal to the political, readers will gain a deeper understanding of the psychological and spiritual landscape of forgiveness from its difficulties to its greatest rewards. With each story are chapters that talk about the different concepts of forgiveness as they relate to each story. The book ends with how forgiveness can be used not only at the individual level but in the political arena as well.

In the process of learning how to forgive, we begin to question all the values and beliefs we hold. Haven't we had enough pain? Perhaps it is through our struggles with our pain that we recognize we can make different choices. It is through these choices that we can change our thinking and change our consciousness, which can ultimately change the world.

-continued-

Nonfiction Sample (continued)

Thank you for your consideration. I look forward to hearing from you.

Sincerely,

Dr. Eileen R. Borris
President, The American Psychological Association
Division 48–Peace Psychology
123-123-1234
authoremail@hotmail.com

Update: Eileen's book has been published by McGraw-Hill under the title, *Finding Forgiveness: A Seven-Step Program for Letting Go of Anger and Bitterness.* There are a number of countries that bought the first version of the book right away at the London Book fair: Germany, Brazil, Japan, Portugal, and Poland. The U.S. only wanted a self-help version, so Eileen wrote a second book proposal and McGraw-Hill snatched it up. According to her agent, there are a number of countries interested in the self-help-only version of the book.)

Nonfiction Sample

---

50 Bible Facts You Need to Know
Before You Get to Heaven

Marion H. Williams
123 Your Street
Anytown, USA

Dear [Literary Agent],

The bestselling success of Mitch Albom's *The Five People You Meet in Heaven* demonstrates that the general public continues to be curious about the afterlife. My book imagines that the afterlife begins with a biblical challenge from St. Peter. He initially welcomes you and acknowledges your strong belief, good works, and generosity. However, in order to pass through the gates of heaven, he requires you to name the four Gospels, locate the Lord's Prayer in the Bible, and quote three scripture passages. Does a blank look come across your face and does sweat start beading up on your forehead?

After attending and teaching numerous Sunday School classes, I became aware that I was not the only one who did not know the Fruits of the Spirit or the names of the twelve disciples off the top of my head. Many of us have a strong faith but lack a working knowledge of the Bible.

The purpose of this book is to give an overview of some important building blocks that most Christians should know but often do not. Furthermore, it is especially important for our children, and especially our teenagers, to know by heart some scripture passages that they can rely on when confronted with peer pressure. By equipping them with this knowledge, they will be better prepared to say "no" and walk away.

-continued-

Nonfiction Sample (continued)

The audience for this book would be primarily nonfundamentalist Christians. Adults, children, and youth would enjoy reading it. This would be a small, pocket-size paperback book that would easily fit in a purse, jacket, or on a bedstand for easy reference. Distribution would be through both Christian and mainstream bookstores.

My manuscript is almost complete. If you would like to see my book proposal, or if you have any questions, please call me at 123-123-1234 or email me at *authoremail@hotmail.com*.

Thank you for your time and consideration.

Sincerely,
Marion H. Williams

Update: Marion's book was published by Recamier Publishing as *Beyond Adam & Eve: 50 Things You Need to Know Before You Get into Heaven (Bible Study Curriculum Guide).*

Nonfiction Sample

The Heart's Way:

For the Recovering Intellectual

Have we become a society of walking heads? Many of us have hidden our true selves and heart's destiny behind a wall of intellectual accomplishments, advanced degrees, self-aggrandizing job titles, or perfectionist personas. The busyness of our lives often prevents us from noticing our heart's voice is screaming out for attention. How many of us work seventeen-hour days six or seven days a week and have little time to spend with our families? Cell phones, e-mail, Blackberrys, and pocket PCs all make us globally available around the clock. We wonder why we have over a 50 percent divorce rate, illness due to job stress, and children fighting for their parent's attention. Now is the time for this book because we are a society that has lost touch with our hearts.

What Julia Cameron's *The Artist's Way* did for awakening the artist within, *The Heart's Way for the Recovering Intellectual* does for the majority of us who have hidden the voice of our heart behind our intellectual accomplishments.

The audience for this book is vast, as it will speak to anyone who wants a greater connection with his or her heart. The book is also for those of us who may remotely identify with being a recovering intellectual. Recovering intellectuals are often found in corporate executive and professional offices and academic institutions, or hiding their true selves behind a myriad of other facades.

Business, corporate, educational, spiritual, and nonprofit organizations as well as ministers, therapists, counselors, doctors, and anyone who loves a recovering intellectual will help promote and popularize this book.

-continued-

Nonfiction Sample (continued)

Lamm walks among the recovering intellectuals with her doctorate from Columbia University, an endless list of other assorted achievements and certifications, and eighteen years of global coaching, consulting, and academic experience working with recovering intellectuals. *Oprah* magazine quoted Dr. Lamm as an expert in personal transformation. She beautifully weaves this expertise into the core foundation of this book.

The book begins with a fun quiz to determine just how much of a recovering intellectual you really are. It is then designed around a thirteen-week program to recover your heart including real-life short stories, transformative exercises, meditations, and specific weekly heart dates that will capture the buried heart of any recovering intellectual. Chapter 1 describes how to use the book, which can be done individually or as part of a support group. The next thirteen chapters are arranged around an acronym that spells "Open Your Heart." Week one is "O" for Opening to Receive; Week two is "P" for Purpose; "E" is for Expression, and "N" for Nurturing, etc. The book concludes with how to integrate your newfound heart connection into your life.

For the "off the charts" recovering intellectual, this book can be read multiple times, uncovering new layers of the heart each time. This book is guaranteed to make a difference in the heart of everyone who reads it. To receive a copy of a proposal along with some sample material or to discuss this project more fully with Sharon, please feel free to contact her at youremail@hotmail.com or 123-456-7890.

Dr. Sharon Lamm

Update: Sharon sent out two different query letters in a four-month period and received over seventy positive replies.

appendix c

Sample Query
Letter Responses from
Literary Agents

Requests for More Information

To: Dr. Sharon Lamm
From: DeFiore and Company

Please send the full proposal for review.

Teresa Hartnett
The Hartnett Agency

To: Dr. Sharon Lamm
From: The Ned Leavitt Agency

Dear Dr. Lamm,

We have received your query letter regarding your two book projects and are interested in seeing more material. Please send a proposal for *THE HEART'S WAY*, and the first 50 pages of *RE-BIRTH THROUGH BIRTH*, along with a SASE to the following address:

The Ned Leavitt Agency
70 Wooster Street
New York, NY 10012

Make sure to include in the cover letter that this is requested material.

Please have patience in hearing back from us. It can take several weeks for us to process material. I assure you that you will hear from us when we have reached a decision on your submission.

Thanks for submitting!

Best,
The Ned Leavitt Agency

To: Dr. Sharon Lamm
From: Sebastian Agency

Dear Dr. Lamm,

While I am not a recovering intellectual, I would very much like to see your proposal package. It makes a lot of sense in theory and could be a wonderful book.

If you have not already committed yourself elsewhere, please send it hardcopy to my attention:

Laurie Harper
Sebastian Agency

To: Dr. Sharon Lamm
From: Natasha Kern Literary Agency

Hi Sharon,

Please do send a copy of your proposal to me (see contact info at bottom). This is exactly right for my list (see that on my website at *www.natashakern.com*)

Warmly,
Natasha

To: Dr. Sharon Lamm
From: Wilson Devereux Company

Dear Dr. Lamm,

BD Barker has given me your submission for review. Are you available for a phone conversation with us Friday, May 12th 2:30 pm est? Please reply with the appropriate telephone number.

Thank You,
Tony Frothingham
VP Acquisitions
Wilson Devereux Company

No Further Materials Requested

To: Anne
From: Harvey Klinger Agency

Thank you for your query. Your project does not sound right for us, but best of luck finding an enthusiastic agent and editor for your work.

In the future, please send your query to queries@harveyklinger.com

For a good idea of the types of projects we represent, we invite you to view our agency website: *www.harveyklinger.com.*

To: Thomas Puetz
From: Shepard Agency

Thank you for thinking of us. However, we are not currently taking on new clients. Have you tried Writers' House at 21 West 26th Street, New York, N.Y.10010; 212-685-2400. Good luck.

The Shepard Agency

To: Paul Hall
From: Mildred Marmur Associates Ltd.

Dear Mr. Hall,

Ms. Lebowitz has decided to leave literary agenting.

Alas, this is a very small agency and the new work of current clients is keeping us over-busy and not able to consider material by new clients.

Your credentials are very impressive and we wish you the best of luck in finding representation, and a publisher, very soon.

Mildred Marmur Associates Ltd.

To: Shirley Hildreth
From: Creative Artists Agency

Dear Ms. Hildreth:

We received your e-mail inquiring about having Creative Artists Agency represent you for the above-entitled project. Although we appreciate your interest, we do not handle publishing at this time, moreover, we have a firm policy of returning all unsolicited material unread. Accordingly, we are forwarding your e-mail back to you and we have deleted your e-mail from our system.

Your unsolicited submission has not been, and will not be disclosed to any executive or other employee of Creative Artists Agency or any other person. You should be aware that many ideas are generated by our employees and our clients or other sources. To the extent that any projects are generated which contain elements similar to what you submitted, the similarities are purely coincidental.

Thank you for considering Creative Artists Agency. We wish you much luck in your endeavors.

Cordially,
CREATIVE ARTISTS AGENCY

appendix d

Sample Nonfiction
Submission Package

A Proposal for

The Heart's Way

Being Good Enough
The Key to Unlocking Inner Peace

OR

The Heart's Way

Do you or someone you know need to get back to who you really
are or discover yourself for the first time?

By Dr. Sharon Lamm-Hartman
PO Box 1234
Yourtown, USA
123-456-7890
author@msn.com
www.insideoutlearninginc.com

Table of Contents

Introduction

What Julia Cameron's, *The Artist's Way* did for struggling artists, *The Heart's Way* does for the recovering intellectual—those of us who have hidden the voice of our heart behind our invented personas, walls of achievements, and busy lifestyles.

We have become a society of walking heads. We have hidden our true selves and heart's destiny behind a wall of accomplishments, advanced degrees, self-aggrandizing job titles, or perfectionist personas. The busyness of our lives prevents us from noticing our heart's voice is screaming out for attention. How many of us work seventeen-hour days six or seven days a week and have little time to spend with our families? Cell phones, e-mail, Blackberrys, and pocket PCs all make us globally available around the clock. We wonder why we have over a 50 percent divorce rate, illness due to job stress and children fighting for their parent's attention. Now is the time for this book because we are a society that has lost touch with our hearts.

There are many books about opening one's heart, but most are associated with a religious orientation and none provide a simple step-by-step approach and transformative program based on years of award-winning research and experience. *The Heart's Way* is the first book to use a simple and profound twelve-week transformative program to recover the hearts of the millions of people who will read and use this book. Thus the audience for this book is vast, as it will speak to anyone who wants a greater connection with his or her heart. The book is also for those of us who may remotely identify with being a "recovering intellectual."

Dr. Sharon Lamm walks among the recovering intellectuals with her doctorate from Columbia University, an endless list of other assorted achievements and certifications, and eighteen years of global coaching, consulting, speaking, and academic experience working with recovering intellectuals like herself. Her research on personal transformation (upon which this book is based) received awards from the Center for Creative Leadership and the Academy of Human Resource Development. *Oprah* magazine quoted Dr. Lamm as an expert in personal transformation. She beautifully weaves this expertise into the core foundation of this book.

A recovering intellectual has one or more of the following characteristics: 1) hides behind academic or professional titles and accomplishments or invented personas, 2) lives such a busy lifestyle there is no time to hear their heart's voice, 3) needs to know too much and express too little, or 4) prefers to analyze and read about life instead of actually experiencing it. Recovering intellectuals are often found in corporate executive and professional offices, academic institutions, or hiding their true selves behind myriad other facades.

Business, corporate, educational, spiritual, and nonprofit organizations as well as ministers, therapists, counselors, doctors, and anyone who loves a recovering intellectual will help promote and popularize this book.

A great addition to the book is that Dr. Lamm is bringing several "recovering intellectuals," including herself, along on the journey as she completes the book. This group will participate in the weekly exercises and e-mail their results and reflections to Dr. Lamm, who will include some of their real-life experiences in the book. Dr. Lamm also has hundreds of client stories who over the years have participated in the exercises in the book. She can draw on any number of these stories to help readers feel they are not alone as they complete the "Heart's Way" program.

The book immediately grabs the readers' attention with a quiz that enables them to determine just how much of a recovering intellectual they really are. Chapter 1 describes a bit about the research and experience upon which the book is based and shares how to use the book, which can be done individually or as part of a support group. The next twelve chapters are the transformative program that will recover readers' hearts. The book structure is arranged around an acronym "Open Your Heart." Week one is "O" for Opening to Receive; Week two is "P" for Purpose; "E" is for Empathy, and "N" for Nurturing, etc. The book concludes with a bonus week "T" for Truth that provides the key to fully commit and decide to live a "Heart's Way" life.

The weekly programs are jam-packed full of real-life short stories, transformative exercises, meditations, and specific weekly "heart dates" that will capture the buried heart of any recovering intellectual. Each week has unique and simple exercises to obtain the lessons for the week's topic. For example, week two, "P" for Purpose, includes an exercise to help readers connect with their unique purpose. This exercise is simple and is already selling on its own as a CD workbook called "Discover Your Life Purpose." The exercises come from years of research and experience on what facilitates personal transformation.

The book will include a folded insert of a poster-sized heart made up of twelve individual heart shapes. At the end of each week, the reader will summarize his or her key learning and takeaways from that week on a weekly summary page inside a dotted-line heart. Each week the reader will cut out the summary page heart and paste it on the poster. This is an interactive way to help readers see and celebrate the progress they are making as they complete the program.

The Heart's Way program can be done multiple times. Each time the reader will uncover yet a deeper layer of his or her heart.

This book will change every aspect of a reader's life, from lifestyle to relationships to chosen careers. Vince, a recovering intellectual client who completed the twelve-week program said, "I was accomplished, financially sound, and extremely depressed. After participating in Dr. Lamm's "Heart's Way" program I met the love of my life, discovered the purpose of my life, and began to live and breathe life as opposed to stumbling through it. This program did more to change my life than anything I have ever done."

Markets for the Book

There are approximately four markets for this book. Those markets are:

1. Business, corporate, and nonprofit executives and professionals who seek to grow beyond the confines of their limited lives (e.g., Those who have read books by such as Tom Peters and Steven Covey in the past);

2. Individuals currently seeking the counsel of therapists, coaches, ministers, and physicians in regard to dealing with depression or unresolved personal issues in their lives;

3. Those who have flocked to and read books such as *The Artist's Way* and *The Purpose-Driven Life*;

4. The spouses, family members, close friends, colleagues, and employers of all of the above.

There is no religious orientation to this book—it is nondenominational. Each human being has a heart, so anyone who wants a greater relationship with his or her heart will love this book. It is an inspiring way to open your heart and is guaranteed to save thousands of dollars in therapy and coaching bills.

Length and Completion Date

The final 80,000-word manuscript will be completed within six months of signing a contract with a publisher.

Spinoffs

The author will write follow-up books:

❑ *Moving into the Heart's Way*—This book will help readers transition into their new life after completing the "Heart's Way" program. It will facilitate long-lasting behavior change.

❑ *Living the Heart's Way*—A collection of stories from people who have made this transition, including descriptions of how their lives are so much better and how they keep living the "Heart's Way" each day.

❑ *Leading to the Heart's Way*—A collection of stories on how readers from the previous books have led others in their lives to take steps to also live the "Heart's Way."

❑ In addition, the author will write complementary books to *The Heart's Way* such as:

❑ *Daily Inspiration for Living a Heart's Way Life: Reflections from the Heart's Way Program* designed to be used as a convenient standalone book for daily reflection or as an easy reference tool when reading *The Heart's Way*. The author will also write customized journals for *The Heart's Way* and each of the above follow-up books.

❑ *The Soul's Way*—A book much like *The Heart's Way* but focused on following one's soul.

Mission Statement

Dr. Lamm's mission is to empower people from all races, belief systems, denominations, and ages to reconnect with their heart and live their divine purpose. This book is the next step. Dr. Lamm has pursued her mission through her award-winning research on personal transformation, speaking engagements, articles and book chapters, media appearances, and her private coaching practice.

Dr. Lamm has a solid platform she can leverage to promote the book and expand its impact. She has designed and delivered thousands of innovative programs and presentations around the world. She has coached hundreds of executives, entrepreneurs, professionals, and CEOs. Through Dr. Lamm's speaking engagements, programs, and coaching she is in front of at least 2,000 executives and professionals each year. Her client organizations include several *Fortune* 500 companies such as GE, Boeing, and American Express. She also teaches at Columbia University and the Center for Creative Leadership and is the director of Central Phoenix Women.

Dr. Lamm has been quoted in *Oprah* magazine as a personal transformation expert and written several journal articles and book chapters on the subject. Her doctorate dissertation on personal transformation received two distinguished awards for its innovative contribution to the field. Dr. Lamm's business was showcased on a Philadelphia local TV program as well as a national cable TV program. She has been featured in the *Phoenix Business Journal*, *Frontdoors* newspaper, *Desert Paradise Magazine*, and several *Who's Who* publications.

Promotional Plan

The author will contribute to the promotion by the publisher in the following ways:

1. **PR budget:** Dr. Lamm will match the publisher's consumer promotion budget up to $30,000.

2. **Media campaign:** Dr. Lamm will hire her own publicist to assist in the efforts of the publisher.

3. **Blog campaign:** Dr. Lamm will direct her publicist under the guidance of the publisher to commence a blog campaign to promote her book.

4. **Tour:** Dr. Lamm and her publicist, in conjunction with the efforts of the publisher, will set up a media/book signing campaign in the following cities: Phoenix, Tucson, San Francisco, San Diego, Los Angeles, Portland, Seattle, New York, Philadelphia, Washington DC, Baltimore, Boston, Chicago, etc. Dr. Lamm and/or her publicist will contact local newspapers, TV, radio stations, and women's organizations in several cities to set up interviews about her book.

5. **PBS:** Dr. Lamm will utilize her already established connections with PBS in Phoenix as well as other PBS stations nationwide to drive promotional opportunities for her book

6. **Teleconference presentations:** Dr. Lamm and her publicist will set up a minimum of 100 teleconference presentations featuring information and promotion on her book.

7. **Seminars and presentations:** Dr. Lamm is in the process of designing specific seminars for the general public under the titles of "The Heart's Way," "Recovering Your Heart," and "Recovering Intellectuals Anonymous." She and her publicist will establish opportunities for her to present these classes at colleges, universities, and organizations.

8. **Organization connections:** Dr. Lamm will also be offering these presentations through a variety of *Fortune* 500 companies and businesses, such as GE's Leadership Development Center, Columbia University, ARCO Chemical Company, Mobil, Exxon, Pepsi, E*TRADE, Stanley Tools, Syngenta, Storecast Merchandising, Fannie Mae, Arizona Society of CPAs, Boeing, American Express, Philadelphia School District, National Association of Women Business Owners—Sedona and Phoenix, Berlex Pharmaceuticals, Volvo Corporation, Holy Cross Hospital, and Fresh Start's Women's Resource Center.

9. **Keynote presentations:** Dr. Lamm will continue her efforts as a keynote presenter at the following professional conferences: The Academy of Human Resource Development; Transformative Learning Conference; Arizona Women's Leadership Forum; etc.

10. **Educational programs:** Dr. Lamm will continue her teaching efforts. She teaches at Columbia University and the Center for Creative Leadership and is the Director for a new Women's Leadership Organization—Central Phoenix Women.

11. **Internet:** Dr. Lamm and her publicist will employ the services of a professional webmaster to design and implement a website that will supplement all of her other promotional efforts. Sharon will integrate the book with her business website *www.insideoutlearninginc.com* and several other websites in organizations that she subcontracts through and has client relationships with, including her client organizations described in #8 and Columbia University. Sharon is well connected and will use these connections to promote her book through website integrations.

12. **Promotional copies:** Dr. Lamm will send more than 150 promotional autographed copies to existing and new media contacts as well as her corporate and organizational clients, universities, and several women's organizations and encourage

them to block-buy books for their employees, members, and others.

13. **Supporting articles (including *O* magazine):** Dr. Lamm will utilize her already strong connection with Martha Beck, who writes for *O* magazine to be potentially featured in that publication as well as *Time, Newsweek, BusinessWeek, Fortune,* and other journals.

14. **Testimonials:** Dr. Lamm will provide endorsements from people (many of whom she has personal connections with) such as: Deepak Chopra, Byron Katie, Marianne Williamson, Oprah, Martha Beck, Madonna, Wayne Dyer, Judith Orloff, Doreen Virtue, Melissa Etheridge, and Hillary and Bill Clinton.

Competing Books

The two international bestselling books that are most similar to *The Heart's Way* are Julia Cameron's *The Artist's Way* and Rick Warren's *The Purpose-Driven Life.*

The Artist's Way is a twelve-week program to recover our artist within. The main subject matter is creativity. *The Heart's Way* is a twelve-week program to recover your heart within. The main subject matter is reconnecting with your heart. Connecting with one's heart is much broader than creativity. *The Heart's Way* is for anyone who has lost touch with their heart and perhaps hidden their heart's authentic voice under a plethora of accomplishments, achievements, invented personas, and workaholic/busy life styles.

Julia Cameron proved that a twelve-week structured self-help program is a bestselling methodology. It is still going strong after ten years on the market. *The Heart's Way* provides a program that is more simple to use, arranged around an acronym "Open Your Heart." One of the criticisms of Cameron's work is that there are just too many tasks to do. It adds to our stressful, busy lifestyles instead of reducing them. Each week, *The Heart's Way* will provide journal exercises, a heart date, real-life stories of people who have completed each program week, and a couple of stretch exercises for the overachieving audience this book will attract. It is incredibly easy and simple to use—its beauty is in its simplicity.

The Purpose-Driven Life is a forty-day structured program that the reader can use to connect with their unique purpose. Again, a structured self-help program proves to make the international bestselling list. However, *The Purpose-Driven Life* is incredibly religious and connected with the Born Again Church. Even with the strong religious overtones of this book, it became a bestseller.

After searching databases of books with "Heart's Way" in the title, most have a religious connotation and none provide a simple program based on years of research and experience. *The Heart's Way* is a nondenominational book. Anyone from any religion will enjoy this book. There are no references to any religion. Each human being has a heart, regardless of their chosen religious orientation.

The Heart's Way is a uniquely powerful simple program that is vastly needed in our busy and "heady" society. It is guaranteed to be an international bestseller.

About the Author

Dr. Sharon Lamm is an award-winning global coach, leadership development consultant, speaker, writer, and educator. She is the president and founder of Inside-Out Learning, Inc., specializing in leadership and personal development, from the heart.

With more than eighteen years of global experience, Sharon has worked across the United States and Europe as well as Beijing, Hong Kong, Singapore, and Thailand for clients such as American Express, GE's Leadership Development Center, Exxon, E*TRADE, ARCO Chemical Company, Mobil Oil Corporation, Berlex Pharmaceuticals, Fannie Mae, Arizona Society of CPAs, Volvo Corporation, Holy Cross Hospital, and Fresh Start Women's Resource Center.

She has designed and delivered thousands of innovative programs and has coached hundreds of CEOs, executives, educators, professionals, and entrepreneurs worldwide. She is currently a preferred executive coach for American Express and Boeing.

In addition to her private practice, consulting, and being on the global lecture circuit, she has published several journal articles and book chapters. She has also produced an audio CD workbook on "Discovering Your Purpose" and is currently writing two books: 1) *Rebirth Through Birth: Rediscovering Yourself Through Motherhood* and 2) *The Heart's Way*.

Dr. Sharon Lamm is dedicated to community stewardship and has served with the Fresh Start Women's Foundation and Arizona State University's Dean's Board of Excellence Mentoring Program. In 2005, she was named as a woman to watch in the *Phoenix Business Journal*. She is the director of a new Women's Leadership Organization – Central Phoenix Women.

Dr. Lamm holds a doctorate from Columbia University in leadership and organization development, a master's in industrial and labor relations from Cornell University, and two bachelor degrees. Sharon has trained as a Life Coach with world-renowned author and life coach teacher, Dr. Martha Beck. She is a Certified Executive and Leadership Coach and a Certified Teacher of the Myers-Briggs Type Indicator.

Dr. Sharon Lamm is an adjunct professor of leadership at Columbia University. She is an adjunct faculty member at the Center for Creative Leadership (San Diego campus), which is consistently rated the #1 leadership development center.

Dr. Lamm has been honored and received awards from the Center for Creative Leadership and the Academy of Human Resource Development for her work and research on personal transformation and leadership development.

She was recently featured in Arizona's local *Desert Paradise Magazine*. She has been quoted on her views of coaching in the July, 2004 edition of Oprah's magazine, *O*.

She lives just outside of Phoenix, Arizona with her husband, James Hartman, and her son Joshua and cat Phoenix.

The Outline: List of Chapters

PART I: Setting Context

Introduction and Quiz

Just How Much of a Recovering Intellectual Are You?

Chapter 1: How to Use This Book to Recover Your Heart

This chapter describes how to use the book and variations for completing the twelve-week program. The book can be done individually or as part of a group with two or more members. It can be completed multiple times, uncovering new layers of one's heart each time. This chapter sets individual and/or group expectations and goals for the program and provides references to the years of research the book is based upon.

PART II: The Twelve-Week Program—"Open Your Heart"

Chapter 2:   "O" – Open to Receive
Chapter 3:   "P" – Purpose
Chapter 4:   "E" – Empathy
Chapter 5:   "N" – Nurturing
Chapter 6:   "Y" – You – Who Are You?
Chapter 7:   "O" – Optimism
Chapter 8:   "U" – Unconditional
Chapter 9:   "R" – Relax
Chapter 10:   "H" – Humility
Chapter 11:   "E" – Expression
Chapter 12:   "A" – Allow
Chapter 13:   "R" – Reach for Your Dreams
Chapter 14:   Bonus Week - T" - Truth

PART III: Integrating Your Newfound Heart Connection into Your Life

Chapter 15:   Now What?

Index

S

T

U

About the Author

Twenty-four years ago, Tom Bird was a publicist with the Pittsburgh Pirates. However, like so many others in the world, at heart he was a writer.

Having applied all the orthodox methods he could get his hands on with little or no results, Tom designed his own method for the writing of a book and getting it published. This system is now referred to as the Tom Bird Method.

Within four weeks of employing his method, Tom landed a literary agent who, at the time, was the most renowned in publishing history. Six weeks later, Tom's first book was sold to Harper & Row, then the third largest publisher in the world. The book sold for a price equivalent to three times his yearly salary as the Assistant Director of Publicity with big league baseball's Pittsburgh Pirates. The sale enabled him to resign from this position and write full-time.

Shortly after Tom's first book was released, he was overwhelmed with calls from aspiring authors wondering how someone so young had done it. Tom responded to their queries by offering a series of classes at local Pittsburgh colleges and universities. Soon, word spread of the simple, direct, and effective methods he taught, creating nationwide demand.

Over the last quarter of a century, Tom has remained committed to sharing his method with writers all across the globe. He has made more than 3,000 lecture appearances before more than 50,000 students at more than 110 different campuses.

"A person should set his goals as early as he can and devote all of his energy and talent to getting there. With enough effort, he may achieve it. Or he may find something that is even more rewarding. But in the end, no matter what the outcome, he will know that he has been alive."

Frequent visitor to Sedona, Walt Disney